THE P

Series Titles

Poetic People Power
Tara Bracco (ed.)

Talking Diamonds
Linda Nemec Foster

The Green Vault Heist
David Salner

There is a Corner of Someplace Else
Camden Michael Jones

Everything Waits
Jonathan Graham

We Are Reckless
Christy Prahl

Always a Body
Molly Fuller

Bowed As If Laden With Snow
Megan Wildhood

Silent Letter
Gail Hanlon

New Wilderness
Jenifer DeBellis

Fulgurite
Catherine Kyle

The Body Is Burden and Delight
Sharon White

Bone Country
Linda Nemec Foster

Not Just the Fire
R.B. Simon

Monarch
Heather Bourbeau

The Walk to Cefalù
Lynne Viti

The Found Object Imagines a Life: New and Selected Poems
Mary Catherine Harper

Naming the Ghost
Emily Hockaday

Mourning
Dokubo Melford Goodhead

Messengers of the Gods: New and Selected Poems
Kathryn Gahl

After the 8-Ball
Colleen Alles

Careful Cartography
Devon Bohm

Broken On the Wheel
Barbara Costas-Biggs

Sparks and Disperses
Cathleen Cohen

Holding My Selves Together: New and Selected Poems
Margaret Rozga

Lost and Found Departments
Heather Dubrow

Marginal Notes
Alfonso Brezmes

The Almost-Children
Cassondra Windwalker

Meditations of a Beast
Kristine Ong Muslim

Praise for
Poetic People Power

"This powerful and nuanced collection of performative verse exemplifies Poetic People Power's impactful use of literary forms to advance social change. The skilled craftsmanship and emotional heft of these works serve as potent reminders of spoken word's transformative potential."

—Daniel Gallant
arts consultant
founder of Litocrat
former executive director at the Nuyorican Poets Cafe

"This book is a revolution unto itself, a 20-year testament to unwavering dedication to poetry and activism, to looking at hard truths and demanding change. Every poem is a gem, and strung together in thematic shows, the poems become prisms through which we get to see different sides of an issue. *Poetic People Power* deserves high praises for this remarkable achievement."

—Chantal Bilodeau
playwright
founding artistic director of Arts & Climate Initiative

"Poets have long used their words for resistance and as mouthpieces for social justice or political movements—José Marti, Julia de Burgos, Pablo Neruda, Gary Snyder, Walt Whitman, Audre Lorde come to mind. The poets in this book are heirs to this tradition—making known those who are unknown, using art to guide our understanding of what could be, and entrusting us with a call to action."

—Elena Martínez
folklorist at City Lore
co-artistic director at Bronx Music Heritage Center

"*Poetic People Power* is a triumph! A testament to how poetry can anchor a calling, a movement. This anthology demonstrates the power of collective voices, how coupling poetry and performance can be in service of something larger than ourselves."

—Deonna Kelli Sayed
writer & performer
chapter leader, PEN America North Carolina Piedmont Region

"Tara Bracco's *Poetic People Power* awakened me to see poets as our true visionary thinkers. Maybe they're not well-known or major influencers, but they are paving the way to create a better world…caring, healing, and problem solving with their stories and poetry. This book inspires me to deeply affirm that goodness will ultimately prevail."

—Meredith Porte
media producer
board member, The Peace Studio

"Poetic is difficult to decipher. People are impossible to understand. Power is at the detriment of us all. *Poetic People Power*, a hybrid theater/literary anthology, is an honest attempt to make sense of why we have so little sympathy for one another. To quote the eloquent poet Amiri Baraka, 'Politics is the gaining & maintaining of Power.' But at what cost? This collection of imagery, metaphor and commitment to peace is a must read for thinking people. It reassures possibilities are endless."

—reg e gaines
poet & Tony Award-nominated playwright
artistic director, Downtown Urban Arts Festival

"Honoring a longstanding, ever growing, powerful tradition of 'speaking truth to power' and telling what must be shared, this work embodies the courage and beauty of poetry, spoken word, story committed and accountable to community, to justice, to change. Exciting, and painful as social truths are, and necessary, Tara Bracco's *Poetic People Power* and the marvelous writers/performers build an irresistible, layered collective call, invitation, insistence to be heard, really heard. And to hear means to be moved to act. Brava to this breathing, singing poetic ensemble reminding us that art is always about connection. And responsibility. That's part of the joy."

—Kathy Engel
poet & cultural worker
author of *The Lost Brother Alphabet* and *Dear Inheritors*
associate arts professor, Department of Art & Public Policy
Tisch School of the Arts, New York University

"I felt so energized by the provocative discourse inspired by the poets' work. It seemed to me that the best of the best were in that room to be heard and recognized as a new generation of performance poets. Thank you for bringing this work to the public. It reminds me of a time in our city where people as a collective cared enough to DO something!"

—Robin Stern
psychologist & author of *The Gaslight Effect*
co-founder & associate director, Yale Center for Emotional Intelligence

"Poetry readings are a decidedly mixed bag: They can be interminable snooze-fests, or, like Wednesday night's show by the folks from Poetic People Power, exciting, engaging, and inspirational."

—Ed Hamilton
contributor, *HuffPost*

"Each spring, some of the fiercest poets are united in New York City to tackle thorny topics—universal health care, voting, democracy—with the power of the spoken word. With wit and fearlessness, they have systematically challenged the status quo, creating a ripple effect."

—Melissa F. Moschitto
Brooklyn Rail

International Human Rights Art Festival
Dixon Place, New York City, March 4, 2017
Photo © Isabella Vi Gomes

Nuyorican Poets Cafe, New York City, December 9, 2017
Photo © Mahir Sufian

Poetic People Power

Three Spoken Word Shows for Social Change

Edited and Created by

Tara Bracco

CORNERSTONE PRESS
UNIVERSITY OF WISCONSIN-STEVENS POINT

Cornerstone Press, Stevens Point, Wisconsin 54481
Copyright © 2024 Tara Bracco
www.uwsp.edu/cornerstone

Printed in the United States of America by
Point Print and Design Studio, Stevens Point, Wisconsin

Library of Congress Control Number: 2023945131
ISBN: 978-1-960329-23-3

"Wasserman Wars with the Wind" copyright © 2019 by Bogar Alonso
"Vote 2020" copyright © 2020 by Suzen Baraka
"WE (must) ACT" copyright © 2021 by Suzen Baraka
"Jane Doe" copyright © 2017 by Tara Bracco
"Earth's Lawyer" copyright © 2019 by Tara Bracco
"A Young Feminist's Journey" copyright © 2020 by Tara Bracco
"I SING" copyright © 2020 by Shanelle Gabriel
"Katarungan" copyright © 2017 by Philippe Javier Garcesto
"Tree of Life" copyright © 2019 by Philippe Javier Garcesto
"War on Women's Bodies" copyright © 2017 by Karla Jackson-Brewer
"FOOOOOD" copyright © 2019 by Karla Jackson-Brewer
"PROTEST" copyright © 2020 by Karla Jackson-Brewer
"Women at Work" copyright © 2020 by Angela Kariotis
"The Danger Isn't Over" copyright © 2017 by Shane Michael Manieri
"HOW" copyright © 2017 by Shetal Shah
"PIONEER" copyright © 2019 by Shetal Shah
"SPEAK" copyright © 2020 by Shetal Shah
"Oyeme Aqui" copyright © 2017 by Natalia Vargas-Caba
"X" copyright © 2021 by Nabil Viñas
"El Sexto" copyright © 2017 by Kesav Wable

I'm No Heroine
Words and Music by Ani DiFranco
Copyright © 1992 Righteous Babe Music
All Rights Administered by Modern Works Music Publishing
All Rights Reserved   Used by Permission
Reprinted by Permission of Hal Leonard LLC

All rights reserved. No part of this book may be reproduced, distributed, or transmitted in any form or by any means, electronic or mechanical, including photocopying or recording, or by an information storage or retrieval system, without the prior written permission of the editor and publisher. All rights, including but not limited to professional performance, amateur performance, recording, motion picture, recitation, lecture, public reading, radio and television broadcasting, podcast, and the right to translate into foreign languages, are expressly reserved. No professional or nonprofessional performance is allowed without prior written permission and appropriate licensing from the copyright holders.

The author expressly prohibits any entity from using this work for purposes of training artificial intelligence (AI) technologies to generate text, including without limitation technologies that are capable of generating works in the same style or genre as this publication. The author reserves all rights to license uses of this work for generative AI training and development of machine learning language models.

Cornerstone Press titles are produced in courses and internships offered by the
Department of English at the University of Wisconsin–Stevens Point.

DIRECTOR & PUBLISHER Dr. Ross K. Tangedal	EXECUTIVE EDITORS Jeff Snowbarger, Freesia McKee
EDITORIAL DIRECTOR Ellie Atkinson	SENIOR EDITORS Brett Hill, Grace Dahl

PRESS STAFF
Carolyn Czerwinski, Kirsten Faulkner, Natalie Reiter, Sophie McPherson, Ava Willett

To all the P3 poets, who showed up to write poems, speak out against injustice, protest, and protect their communities—even when there was little time to write, when bills overflowed, when the news was suffocating, when family issues overwhelmed. You showed up. To create new art, to demonstrate that words matter, and to inspire people to change the world.

Contents

Foreword by Karla Jackson-Brewer   xv
Introduction by Tara Bracco   xxi

The Eco Rise   1
Can You Hear Me Now?   41
While We Were Sleeping   85

Notes   129
Contributors   137
Stay Active!   143
Acknowledgments   147

Foreword

I met Tara Bracco in 2004 through the Woodhull Institute for Ethical Leadership, where I served as board member and teacher. At that time, it had been many years since I had written a poem. In the early 1980s, I belonged to a writers' collective in Brooklyn, NY: Gap Tooth Girlfriends, founded by poet and writer Alexis De Veaux. We attended writing workshops and worked on poetry together, then created an anthology in 1981 called *Gap Tooth Girlfriends*.

Then I became a mother. Raising three children in New York City takes a lot of energy and focus. Years passed with only snippets of incomplete poems and essays. In April 2007, I found myself in the audience at the Bowery Poetry Club, mainly to support Tara as a colleague as she presented a Poetic People Power show. It was my first time attending one of her annual events, and I didn't expect to feel so empowered by the poets' words. But as I listened to each poet present their poems about the need for universal health care, in a show titled *Sick & Tired*, I was impressed by the connections made in their work. I was reminded of just how potent words and poetry can be and the importance of writing our experiences. During intermission, I was so inspired that I crafted a poem about police violence and the shootings of Sean Bell and Amadou Diallo on some receipts in my purse. I scrawled the refrain "50 bullets, 41 bullets to end the life of a Black Man" across the thin slips of paper.

Listening to the poets and their different styles awakened an artistic part of me that had been silent for years. I've long been an activist for social change in the anti-violence movement, speaking out against inequality in our society, but something about that presentation rekindled a creative voice in me that said, "You can do this, so start doing it." I continued going to the Poetic People Power shows each year, and as Tara and I continued to work together professionally, our friendship grew.

Several years later, Tara and I were waiting on line together to see a show at the Public Theater when I mentioned that her project had inspired me to write again. The next year, in 2012, she invited me to be one of 13 poets in the group's anniversary show *Retro-Active: 10 Years of Poetic Action*. It was the first time I'd ever had my writing commissioned. I went from being an audience member at her shows to getting paid to write and present my work at the Helen Mills Theater in midtown Manhattan. As the years passed, I became a returning poet with the project, performing in a total of 10 of 20 annual shows.

One of the things I appreciate about Tara's leadership is that she intentionally invests in an ever-enlarging pool of poets across age, race, class, orientation, and life experience, resulting in deeply enriched work. For twenty years, she's been giving poets an experience of true collaboration rooted in respect and admiration that creates a unique camaraderie.

After writing our poems and weeks before a performance, we gather to read them aloud and receive feedback from the group. Open critique can be harrowing, but Tara has created an atmosphere where poets engage in a fun and playful way, eagerly sharing what worked well in the poems and offering suggestions with our best possible work in

Foreword

mind. We often entered those rehearsal rooms as strangers and left as enthusiastic champions of one another's work.

Poetic People Power is about much more than poetry. The shows are not something you simply listen to. All the poems have hooks; they have tentacles that reach into the audience members' minds to raise questions, pull at their empathy, and invite them to think of solutions. The work truly marries poetry and social change in a rare and remarkable way.

This is part of Tara's genius. She finds talented, emerging poets to write about the issues that affect us as a society. She shines the spotlight on sites of rupture, harm, or injustice in our world and encourages everyone to take the next actions available to them. At the back of every Poetic People Power program is a list of resources poets and audiences can use to make concrete choices that shift the world toward a better future.

Tara's deep dedication to activism roots her in the long lineage of poets and organizers whose work held their societies accountable and nurtured dreams of what could be. With her vast and focused vision, she works beyond the boundaries of the page or written word.

For 44 years, I've lived on the Lower East Side of New York City, an area known for being a hub of art and activism. The neighborhood around me has long been the home of esteemed institutions like La MaMa, The Poetry Project at St. Mark's Church, Theater for the New City, and the Clemente Soto Vélez Cultural & Education Center. In this time, I've attended countless artistic events, and I can say that Tara is one of the best producers in New York City. Not only does she commission this work and invest in artists, she also places the shows in high-quality venues in front of an audience that respects the work and, year after year, shows up to listen and learn. Every Poetic People Power audience includes people who have never attended a poetry reading before, or who have never considered themselves an activist. Initially, they come to support Tara or an individual poet, and then leave with their minds and hearts expanded and exposed to new ideas. In doing so, she cultivates a respectful, thoughtful, and activated audience, allowing us to grow as artists, take more risks, and dream bigger for our work.

As a powerhouse producer, Tara also broadened this dream for us by cultivating relationships with business contacts and other producers, creating opportunities—including this anthology—that would not exist without her innovation and skill. As a result of working with Poetic People Power, I've also been paid to present my poems in other venues.

In this anthology, three recent shows are published for the first time, giving poetry lovers, activists, teachers, and students outside of New York City access to our work. The book includes three of our shows: *The Eco Rise*, about environmental heroes; *Can You Hear Me Now?*, about women's voices; and *While We Were Sleeping*, about human rights abuses. I'm proud to have my work included in these shows and in this book, along with 11 other writers who came together with wide-ranging styles to share timely messages that inform and inspire.

As an educator, I look forward to introducing students to these poems as accessible examples of how much power words have, even in our everyday language. They illustrate how to use words to take a reader or listener on a journey that imparts a sense of liberation. The work included in this book offers an exciting encounter with language, conveys an array of artistic perspectives, and touches on themes and issues that impact people of all ages.

Throughout the project's two-decade history, the work was prophetic, often covering subjects many months before

Foreword

the issues addressed became a part of national consciousness and conversation. With her intuitive early recognition of issues vital to our modern human experience, Tara has always been ahead of her time. Because of this, the poems created through this project have the momentum to propel readers into the future.

On a personal level, the ten years that I've been a part of Poetic People Power have given me the opportunity to write pieces on many social and political topics. I'm most proud of the poems: "Booyaka, Booyaka" about gun violence, for the show *Not Yet Said*, and "Whoosh/Breathe/Pause" for the show *Take Your Time*, speaking to work-life balance. These poems wouldn't have existed without Poetic People Power. Writing a commissioned piece on an assigned topic held me to a higher level of accountability, creativity, and clarity in my work. And yet, I also felt free and safe enough to try new modalities, new word patterns, and new imagery in my poems.

But most importantly, this project has encouraged me to proclaim my identity as a writer. Over four decades after my poetry was first published in an anthology, I am published in an anthology again, thanks to Tara Bracco and Poetic People Power. At the end of our shows we, the poets, ask the audience, "What art will you make? What action will you take?"

Allow this anthology to spark your imagination, free your voice, and transform you into a change agent in the world.

—Karla Jackson-Brewer, MS
Women's, Gender, and Sexuality Studies | Africana Studies
Rutgers University
New York City
June 2023

Introduction

In 2003, I gathered a group of poets at the activist bookstore Bluestockings on the Lower East Side of Manhattan in New York City. The event, titled *Women's Words About War*, was inspired by the Poets Against the War movement, in response to the Iraq War. What began as one evening of poetry grew into an art and social change project, named Poetic People Power, which went on to present 20 spoken word shows about the issues of our time. 2023 marks Poetic People Power's 20th anniversary.

Poetic People Power uses the expressive art of poetry to explore social and political topics, offering insights and solutions to issues that affect our everyday lives. Our shows have been presented to many hundreds of people in theaters, cafes, colleges, and festivals. The project has long been a space for amplifying diverse voices, culturally and aesthetically. In many ways, Poetic People Power is a microcosm of what art and activism looks like in New York City.

The forming of the project was the result of many personal and professional experiences.

I wrote poetry as a child, and when I was 15 years old, I was published for the first time. My poem "Take Me Home"—written during the Gulf War in 1991, from the perspective of a soldier—was printed in the Long Island newspaper *Newsday*. Even as a teenager, I was using poetry to address the issues happening in the world around me. I

Introduction

continued scribbling poems on papers and typing them out on my word processor while I attended Marymount Manhattan College, where I studied theater and speech-language pathology to combine my interests in language, communication, and performance.

There was a special poetic energy in New York City in the mid-1990s. I attended downtown poetry readings featuring poets Asha Bandele, Jessica Care Moore, and Tony Medina at venues like the Public Theater and Wetlands, and I discovered slam poetry at the Nuyorican Poets Cafe. As a young, feminist artist, I found poetry more empowering than theater. With poetry, I could write my own pieces and workshop them immediately. I didn't have to audition or wait for someone else to decide if I was good enough to participate. It was validating, but I still didn't feel like there was a space for my voice because my writing didn't fit neatly into literary or slam poetry, the two scenes that dominated at that time.

So, after I graduated college and outstayed my welcome sleeping on a friend's floor, I self-funded my own cross-country poetry tour, traveling for two months alone by bus and train to read my work at open mic nights in cities including Chicago, Seattle, and San Francisco. The experience allowed me to see how many other people were writing and presenting poetry that wasn't easily defined, but equally powerful and deserving to be heard. I returned to New York City with an even greater sense that the existing poetry scenes weren't expansive enough for the range of work that was being created.

The founding of Poetic People Power six years later was influenced by the democratization of the slam scene and driven by a punk, Do-It-Yourself ethos. My friends were

Introduction

(and still are) punks, artists, and activists. In our 20s, we found work in low-paying nonprofit jobs, critiqued neoliberalism in book clubs, and spent what little money we had left at the end of the week on music festivals.

As my personal experiences drew me to the art form of spoken word, my professional experiences taught me how to be a better writer and produce shows.

All my early jobs were working for theaters and feminist companies. I worked part-time as an assistant to poet and novelist Erica Jong, which was like a crash course in women's studies and writing. Erica was the first person to give me a sense that a woman could have a career as a writer and have influence. At the off-Broadway theater Women's Project & Productions (now named WP Theater), I worked under legendary founder Julia Miles, where I learned the many elements that go into producing theater and running a nonprofit organization. Watching Julia in the early 2000s advocate for women to have a rightful presence in theater was hugely influential. I also worked alongside esteemed women leaders in their respective fields at the Woodhull Institute for Ethical Leadership, teaching leadership skills to thousands of young women across the country. Woodhull, which ceased its programs in 2012, encouraged women to get their writing published, helped position women as experts, and created a community among women to help each other succeed in their careers.

Today, young people have platforms to be heard publicly. They can post their opinions on social networking sites, blog their ideas online, and connect with others through their own newsletters. It's easy to forget that in 2003, when I was a young writer starting Poetic People Power, the world was very hierarchical. I didn't have connections or training from an Ivy League school. There was no social media. I knew little about the publishing world, which felt like a closed society. If I wanted to keep writing and keep growing artistically, I had to find my own way and develop my own community. I had to create the answers to my own questions.

The questions that kept resurfacing for me at that time were: How can I continue to carve out time to write and be an activist, on top of a demanding day job? How can I educate myself about the complexities of the issues around us that operate as the undercurrent of our lives? How can I develop as a writer when there is no pathway for my work, when no one is paying me to write, when no one is encouraging me to keep going?

Poetic People Power grew out of these reflections. I made a commitment to myself and my community to produce a show that would combine poetry and activism once a year; a show that required me to research a particular issue and write about it. And I knew this needed to be done with other artists. This couldn't be a one-woman show, especially if I was serious about social change. The work needed to be done in good company, with other emerging artists and talented changemakers.

I aimed to create a space where marginalized voices could rise up together and be appreciated individually. I also wanted to push the boundaries of the art form and include a range of voices and poetry styles. I borrowed from the theater and publishing world by offering poets commissions for their work because I felt strongly that it was essential to developing talent. The same way I was paid to write for independent publications like *Clamor*, *BUST*, and *Bitch* when I was an emerging journalist with few writing clips, I paid emerging poets. This was unheard of. Poets today still

Introduction

pay fees in order to submit their work for consideration to publications and contests.

For 20 years, I've presented spoken word shows that premiered the commissioned poems to the public on downtown stages, including Nuyorican Poets Cafe, Bowery Poetry Club, Wild Project Theater, Theatre 80, and Caveat. I presented the work in reputable spaces where the poets could be heard and appreciated, without the distractions that can happen in a bar or bookstore. Volunteering my time, I created and produced each show—from start to finish—choosing show themes, researching topics, crafting titles and marketing copy, auditioning talent, securing venues, and writing scripts. I secured small grants to offset production costs, and through targeted marketing efforts, I built an audience for this work, with people returning year after year to hear from our artists.

Over the years, the shows covered a range of social and political topics, including inequality, universal health care, human rights violations, climate change, the global water crisis, time poverty, and gentrification. Often, we presented these shows before mainstream media coverage of the topics. Our 2005 show on global warming was presented a year before Al Gore's film *An Inconvenient Truth* was released; our 2007 show about the need for universal health care premiered before Barack Obama was elected president; our 2011 show about revolution took place four months before Occupy Wall Street; and our 2013 show about inequality was presented at the start of the Black Lives Matter movement.

Our society is finally having conversations about social justice, diversity, equity, and inclusion, which are long overdue. When I started Poetic People Power, there were few funders supporting art and social change, and it was a challenge to get people to recognize the value of this project. I was told too many times that art shouldn't be political. That, to me, seemed like a privileged perspective, an unaffected worldview while these issues were playing out in people's lives. I knew that the topics of our shows weren't just political issues to be debated within the walls of Washington, D.C.; they were affecting the well-being of our lives and we needed a collective space to understand and process the issues, and give voice to people's lived experiences. While poets were commissioned to write on a specific theme, they were given creative freedom and weren't required to write advocacy poems; instead, there was a focus on how the issue affected them personally.

Poetic People Power uses poetic storytelling on stage to educate and inspire audiences, but we are not a theater group. We operate in the spoken word space. In early years of the project, I emceed the shows and provided a narrative in between each poets' presentation, providing a throughline to connect the pieces, informing the audience about the complexities of the topic, and offering solutions and action steps. In later years, I structured the shows more like theater pieces—with opening and closing scenes that included the full group, and individual scenes in the middle written by the artists—and the commissions were more research based.

In this anthology, three of our recent shows are published for the first time. The book includes shows about environmental heroes, women's voices, and human rights abuses. The shows are: *The Eco Rise, Can You Hear Me Now?*, and *While We Were Sleeping*. The anthology includes work from 12 diverse artists with a range of writing styles.

The storytelling within these pages largely reflects how the artists presented their work in our live shows. Poems

Introduction

have been edited for clarity, and in one case, restructured. In the editing process, I focused on readability, giving each poet the room and flexibility to present their spoken pieces on the page as they wanted them to be represented. To help guide the reader, I included stage directions to give a greater sense of how these pieces were intended to be presented. The individual scenes, written by the poets, reflect their creativity, and in some cases their own opinions, with the author indicated at the top of each scene.

It might be tempting to read the poems individually or out of order, but I encourage readers to read the book as it's been put together to experience the narrative arc of each show and the power of collective storytelling. This will also allow readers a chance to read production notes and content warnings before experiencing the shows.

While the project has received grant awards and some local and national press, the grassroots work of Poetic People Power is largely unknown outside of New York City. With this publication, our work is now available to a wider audience.

My hope is that readers will learn from these poetic shows and feel moved enough to seek solutions to the issues that impact their own lives and the community around them. After 25 years of working in the nonprofit sector, including two decades leading this poetry project, I know that real change is possible.

Following our spoken word shows, audience members have told me that they have volunteered at nonprofits, participated in protests, donated to causes, changed their consumption habits, and written their own poems. I personally was so moved by what I learned from our 2009 show, *Tapped Out*, about the global water crisis, that I cofounded an

Introduction

international nonprofit organization, The Project Solution, with my long-time friend Joe Gonzalez; the organization is now serving 30,000 people in 14 countries.

Art fosters connection, and information moves people to action. The word audiences use the most to describe a Poetic People Power show is "inspiring." When I began the project, I sensed that poetry could be an entry point for people to begin exploring social and political issues and what we could do about them. And I was steadfast in that mission, creating the space I long wished someone else had created for my own work.

Now two decades later, I've created and produced 20 spoken word shows, commissioned 130 poems, and worked with 40 poets. There is no other group like Poetic People Power in the country that has continually commissioned new work by poets on the topics of our time and premiered that work annually to the public through professional spoken word shows.

A phrase used among activists years ago when I started Poetic People Power was "another world is possible." For me, another world is possible with poetry.

—Tara Bracco
Producing Artistic Director
Poetic People Power
New York City
July 2023

The Eco Rise

The Eco Rise

— Production Note —

The Eco Rise was presented live on Zoom on Earth Day on April 22, 2021. Tara Bracco created and produced the show to shine a spotlight on environmental heroes who have worked in their communities—either locally or at the international level—to advocate for the well-being of people and the planet.

The show includes original poetic pieces by Bogar Alonso, Suzen Baraka, Tara Bracco, Philippe Javier Garcesto, Karla Jackson-Brewer, Shetal Shah, and Nabil Viñas. The public presentation included guest artists Anish Jethmalani, presenting Alonso's poem and his lines in the group scenes, and poet Erica R. DeLaRosa in Bracco's poem as the voice of the 911 phone operator.

Funding was made possible by the Puffin Foundation.

— Producer's Note —

Poets were commissioned to research and write about an environmental hero who is not a household name. We aimed to present works on a range of local and international environmentalists who are working to address different issues, including deforestation, ecocide, environmental racism, and pollution. For continuity purposes, poets were encouraged to name the person they were writing about in their poem, use poetic storytelling, and be creative but truthful as they penned stories of these environmental leaders.

Creative work on this show began in March 2019. We hoped to coproduce a show for the stage with Poetic Theater Productions, but the COVID-19 pandemic changed our plans. Instead, the show was presented live over Zoom by

Poetic People Power during the pandemic while theaters were shut down. Through their Poetic Open Sessions in 2019, Poetic Theater Productions provided a space for three of our artists to workshop early drafts. On September 15, 2019, poets Shetal Shah and Bogar Alonso presented their poems from this show as invited artists at the 2019 Climate Change Theatre Action launch event, which took place in Manhattan at Caveat, coproduced by The Arctic Cycle and Poetic People Power.

The Eco Rise

SCENE 1
Unknown Heroes
Written by Tara Bracco

Lights up on poets.

SHETAL:
I didn't know his name, but I felt his power

BOGAR:
I didn't know her name, but she changed my world

KARLA:
I didn't know her work until she won awards

TARA:
I didn't know her history until I read her book

PHILIPPE:
I didn't know him

SUZEN:
I didn't know her

NABIL:
I didn't know
that before they were known
they did work
that was worthy of being known

SHETAL:
Before people are known
they do work
worthy of being known

SUZEN:
These are the people who are changing our world

BOGAR:
As fires rage
As earthquakes crack open the earth
As droughts scorch the land

NABIL:
As pollution clouds the sky
As plastic floats in oceans
As animals become extinct

TARA:
There are people working, advocating, hoping
In communities throughout the world
Putting vision into action

PHILIPPE:
So that we can live longer, healthier
So that our planet can survive

KARLA:
They do this work

SUZEN:
Before people are known
they do work
worthy of being known

PHILIPPE:
They do this work

SHETAL:
Before people are known
they do work
worthy of being known

KARLA:
They do this work
Not for book deals or Nobel Prizes
Not for recognition on international stages
Not for huge grants or monetary awards

TARA:
But because they know
If they don't act now
There will be a time when we can no longer act

BOGAR:
These are the stories
Of people whose names are not widely known

PHILIPPE:
These are the stories
Of the work they've done

TARA:
These are the stories
That inspire us all to do our part

KARLA:
To show up for our communities

SUZEN:
To make change

NABIL:
To dream big

SHETAL:
And to create a better world
Right now

Lights out.

SCENE 2
Wasserman Wars with the Wind
Written by Bogar Alonso

An image of Kimberly Wasserman along with her name is projected on a screen prior to the poem.

Lights up.

BOGAR:

You know war had come to Chicago
when mothers at picnics
began to sound like battalion commanders.
Saying,

The air in these parts kills.
Slowly, but it kills.
It kills...

In Chicago,
all eyes were glued to the TV and to the bullets.
Bullets and TV.
TV and bullets.
When they should have been glued to the wind.

The wind, the breeze, the air—
Kimberly Wasserman
could hear, see them killing
her boy.

Choking him,
ballooning him,
fattening him for the slaughter.

Poetic People Power

Kimberly Wasserman
didn't know much about
taking on councilmen,
captains of industry,
or bigwigs in big suits,
but she did know that
little boys shouldn't have to go to war
with their own breath.

They shouldn't have to go to war with
230 pounds of mercury,
17,000 tons of nitrogen oxide,
260,000 pounds of soot.

They shouldn't have to go to war with
230 pounds of mercury,
17,000 tons of nitrogen oxide,
260,000 pounds of soot.

In Chicago's two Mexican neighborhoods,
coal-powered plants used to rain down
230 pounds of mercury,
17,000 tons of nitrogen oxide,
260,000 pounds of soot
every year.

Coal-powered.
Like clockwork.
Like the devil's work.
Like snow on Christmas.
Coal-powered.

Some Chernobyl shit.

The Eco Rise

At first,
Wasserman's community had confused the smokestacks—
puffing out white marshmallows—for scenery.
Kids even called them cloud factories.
Seeing in them
Saturday morning cartoons.
Seeing in them
a childhood canvas.
Seeing in them
grandfathers smoking pipes next to cats, fat on love.

But the emergency visits,
the coughing fits,
her son's blue lips,
the wheezing, the wheezing, the WHEEZ-ING
told a different story.
A sad story.

Coal-powered.

The word
"coal-powered"
had told her the story
Wasserman needed to know.
In America,
some boys can breathe,
and some cannot.

"Coal-powered."
Even the word sounds like it's choking on itself.

Men like Donald Trump, Jr.
laugh at the idea that air can be racist.

Poetic People Power

That air can kill.
And yet,
here were neighborhoods of people dying,
being told their deaths were an inconvenient truth.

But Wasserman would have none of that.

Mothers have gone to war for far less.
Seeing no humor in the wind being made to betray her
in her city of wind,
she took up arms against the smokestacks and the fat stacks,
leading an army of Chicago mothers in the fight to
reclaim breathing.

She went from at-home mom
to at-war activist,
knocking on doors,
and knocking them down too.
For ten years she fought,
until factories
pulled the plug on themselves,
going up in a cloud of smoke,
a puff of irony not lost on her.

Her boy could breathe again,
even if not the same ever gain.

His mom had done it.

Kimberly Wasserman warred with the wind
and won.

Lights out.

SCENE 3
PIONEER
Written by Shetal Shah

An image of Pablo Solón Romero along with his name is projected on a screen prior to the poem.

Lights up.

SHETAL:

Amidst the sea of all the seas
And within the trees of all the trees,
A lone voice cried—"Los Derechos de la Madre Tierra."
Pablo Solón cried—"Harmony with Nature"
and "Rights of Indigenous Peoples."
Over and over he cried.
Son of Bolivia's cherished muralist,
Pablo Solón Romero
Came from a certain name
Could've ridden the wave
Of his father's fame.
It would've been easy-peasy
To drift lazily with the breeze
To ride out the glory and the prestige
Afforded by sustaining the status quo
So eagerly established by Western politicos.
But to go gently with the flow,
And ebb with the tide,
Allowing money over matter to run the show—
Not his style.
Like a torrent, he blew open the possibilities
for true diplomatic mobility

Poetic People Power

When in 2009 he was chosen to represent his Bolivian country
at the United Nations overseas.
He stood as strong as an oak among a forest of weeds.
I was lucky, I was a member of one of his teams.
He was a short man, but he seemed like a goliath to me.
Armed with the *Vivir Bien* philosophy—
A philosophy that values non-human entities equally,
A philosophy that alters radically the dominant paradigm of progress,
A philosophy that finds the balance within development and Nature—
He tried and tried
To channel care and love
Over a monetary price.

A tsunami swelled within his throat,
"La Madre Tierra," he continued to cry.
As he approached his seemingly diplomatic United Nations peers,
He strived to make strides beyond the backwoods
of predatory, predetermined politics;
To create a new society that values Big Momma
Without the need to attach a price tag on her gifts.
Yet, the ears he battered with the whipping winds of his voice
Shut out his ideals faster than a bolt of lightning.
A lone man, he howled
Amongst a flock of tepid sheep too consumed
with capitalist consumption,
Too far gone to stop the charades and strategy games hidden inside
Pocket vests and A-line dresses.
Too complacent behind the confines of their comfy chairs
To see that the view just outside their large-scale windows
Reflects corruption and despair.
So, this pioneer circumnavigated his United Nations peers,
Set ablaze his dissatisfaction at their denial of Mother Earth's rights
And gathered outside voices keen to magnify

The Eco Rise

A "systemic alternative" to the crisis that faces humanity.
From the eye of this tornado's frenzy emerged the first
World People's Conference on Climate Change
and the Rights of Mother Earth.
What I like to call the Bolivian anti-UN climate change,
climate change gathering.
In 2010, Pablo led us
To a truly democratic brainstorm of forward action,
Forever documented in history.
He remains as bold, determined, kind and ever true to his *Vivir Bien* beliefs,
Even though it meant breaking thick bonds with Evo, his president,
And becoming the target of his own government.
He remains always on the side of protecting Indigenous lives
and preserving acres of nature.
Preserving Pachamama.
Because our bonds to Mama are the strongest there are.

Lights out.

SCENE 4
WE (must) ACT
Written by Suzen Baraka

An image of Peggy Shepard along with her name is projected on a screen prior to the poem.

Lights up.

SUZEN:

For people of color, breathing is an act of revolution.
So pollution is how they put their knees on our necks
without breaking a sweat,
like asthma ain't the R&B version of COVID,
with low-income minorities being disproportionately affected.

Harlem, did you know you were a sacrifice zone?
The home of MTA bus depots, a sewage treatment plant,
parking lots where parks should be,
with the highest rates of pediatric asthma in all of New York City.
That is, until Martin Luther King Day 1988
when Peggy Shepard stopped traffic
on the West Side Highway, got arrested,
and in 1992 sued the MTA.
Sometimes heroes save lives generations in advance.
$55 million to retrofit the North River Sewage Plant.
There will be children born in West Harlem
who will never feel the MTA's hands wrapped around their ribs
because thanks to Peggy Shepard,
every NYC bus was replaced with a hybrid.

The Eco Rise

WEACT is the West Harlem Environmental Action non-profit
started by Ms. Shepard dedicated to giving low-income
communities of color the tools to advocate for better.
WEACT when they turn our rivers into dumping grounds
because they think we have less political impact.
WEACT when they turn our parks into high-rises
because they think we are unfamiliar with their procedures.
WEACT when they turn our towns into cancer grounds
because the land is cheaper.
WEACT when they turn our schools into cesspools
because they think we don't vote.
WEACT because the world is burning, the climate is turning,
and Black bodies are under attack.

Now East New York is smoking and the Bronx is choking
on that same rancid truth:
that to them, we ain't nothing but sophisticated balloons.
But the joke's on them, because balloons can fly,
defy gravity when they're not oppressed at the neck by a string or a tether,
so imagine if princesses in Queens were allowed to breathe unfettered.
Global warming is much more than a change in the weather.
A breath of fresh air should not be hard to come by.
I wonder if they're scared, that if we fill our lungs with enough of the sky,
we'll reclaim our magic and remember how to fly.

I smell racism lingering in the breeze,
but as Peggy is my shepherd, we must act,
and follow her lead.

Lights out.

SCENE 5
Tree of Life
Written by Philippe Javier Garcesto

An image of Sebastião Salgado along with his name is projected on a screen prior to the poem.

Lights up.

PHILIPPE:

Imagine in thousands

Sebastião Salgado with an eye for the future
2,700,000 trees planted in 20 years

Photojournalist, environmentalist
Journeying across continents and settling back in his
   homeland of Brazil
He set out to bring life back into the region of his youth

"The big problem with our species," he said, "is that when we live a long time, it's only a hundred years. We can't imagine in thousands of years."

In his years, friends disappeared and were targeted
   one by one in the wake of Brazil's 1964 military coup
The dictatorship shut down dissent and the social and
   progressive actions of his peers
For raising their voices and calling out the injustices
   committed by the government

The Eco Rise

Forced to flee from Brazil, Sebastião and his wife, Lélia, settled
  in free Paris
It was here he acquired his Pentax Spotmatic II with a
  50-millimeter lens
Flicking the f-stop and playing with the aperture,
  a spark unlocked

Nossa!

Taking up his calling with photography
He became one of the most iconic social documentarians
  of the 20th century
Swept up major awards in photojournalism capturing in black and white
Beauty and suffering, focused on stories of migration, globalization,
  and greed

He then set his lens on the plight of his own people
After the fall of the military dictatorship
He returned home to Brazil
Where peasant farmers were working to reclaim
  the corporate controlled farmland
He documented the Landless Workers Movement
And the traditional tribal lands of the Awa and Yanomami people
As miners and loggers invaded

It was in this setting that Sebastião and Lélia's greatest contribution
  to our world was manifested

The family farm of his youth that once yielded
  a voluminous forest was gone
The "bare crust" in Minas Gerais had long lost her trees
Her soil overrun with invasive cattle grass
Lélia thought, "Why not plant?"

Poetic People Power

Their Instituto Terra was born

From 100,000 seedlings in methodical pace on primed land
A seedling every 10 feet moving across 2,000 trees per hectare
Planting legumes and Brazilian fire trees to enrich the soil

In following years they increased their efforts and their gains grew
The trees nurtured healthy soil capturing precipitation and water
Despite the dry season birds sang and water flowed

As life blossomed and returned to the region, he imagined again

Turned his eye towards documenting
Bridging environmental action with art
Creating his photo essay *Genesis*, capturing the wild nature across the ends of the Earth

A worldwide cultural movement
A reflection of his life
A journey to Instituto Terra

2,700,000 trees planted in 20 years

Imagine in thousands

Lights out.

SCENE 6
X
Written by Nabil Viñas

An image of Xiuhtezcatl Martinez along with his name is projected on a screen prior to the poem.

Lights up.

NABIL:

Water, Fire, Earth, Air
From the Aztec tradition a child will lay bare
What's at stake
The original caretakers of the land
For my future and yours, he'll take a stand

I acknowledge that I am standing on Ohlone land
Xiuhtezcatl Martinez stands on a 40-generation lineage
Mesoamerican people of Central Mexico
The Aztecs

His name
Shoe-tez-caht

Water, Fire, Earth, Air
And this child from here or there will prepare the unaware

Born to a father who said all life was sacred
Xiuhtezcatl was raised by Siri Martinez in the Mexica tradition
A native people of Mexico

Echoes
Of a people who've been here

Poetic People Power

Echoes of a people who have persevered
Echoes of a people who are still here
Xiuhtezcatl

Agua, Fuego, Tierra, Aire
Cuidas, Lucha, Canta, Baile

His first language was Spanish
But he gave thanks to the natural elements
With a prayer in his native Nahuatl language
He did this to open his first public
Speech on the environment
He was 6 years old
Xiuhtezcatl said the Earth was sacred
Said Mother Earth was alive

Water, Fire, Earth, Air
Mother Earth is alive and his mother provided care

His mother Tamara Roske crouched behind him
As he gave his speech at age 6
And she founded an international
Environmental conservation organization
Xiuhtezcatl would become youth director of this group
The Earth Guardians

What does a child have to offer us?
What could he know?
He knew we were all connected
And that we depend on the elements to survive
"Protect The Sacred" would be the phrase on a sticker
He'd slap onto his laptop as a teenager
With long hair, he moves, he dances, he sings
He kicks a rhyme

The Eco Rise

Water, Fire, Earth, Air
He gave thanks to the elements, the president gave him theirs

Xiuhtezcatl was 13 when he was awarded the U.S. Volunteer Service Award by then President Barack Obama
He was the youngest of 24 national change-makers chosen
To serve on the President's Youth Council

Water, Fire, Earth, Air
Triple Dare Multilingual Sharp Remarks Shared

Age 15, he addressed the United Nations General Assembly
In three languages
He said, "What's at stake right now is the existence of my generation...and the continuation of the human race."

He said, "We are approaching 21 years of United Nations Climate Talks and...almost no agreements have been made on a bonding climate recovery plan."

"We need to reconnect with the Earth," he said.
"We are all connected," he said.
Xiuhtezcatl

Water, Fire, Earth, Air
When a child breathes through truth, he may even file suit

Sharp truths
He spoke them
You'd hear him at a rally
You'd see him at a march

Poetic People Power

La Lucha
He brought it
To those in the spotlight
To those sitting in the dark

Xiuhtezcatl
Dared to bring it to DC
Dared to bring it to the suits and pros
And he dared to bring it to those wielding gavels in black robes

Again at age 15, for a cause most supreme
Xiuhtezcatl joined 20 other youth in filing a lawsuit
Against the United States Government
The suit formally charged the country with
Failing to act on climate change

Fire, Fire, Fire
They sought an injunction ordering the government to
Implement a plan to phase out fossil fuel emissions
Draw down CO_2
He was 15

Earth
In 2016, the U.S. tried to throw this case out
A federal judge denied that motion
Juliana v. United States continues today

Air
As it bounces around federal courts
Xiuhtezcatl bounces to his beats
With moves and with a movement
With millions marching the streets

The Eco Rise

Like the Global Climate Strike of 2019

What do children have to offer us?
What could they know?
Perhaps they are closer to the Earth like they are closer to their birth
Perhaps they see their futures stretching out longer than ours
And they see what's at stake, what it takes
And that we may be out of hours

Power
Pa'lante
The strikers continue

Water
We're on a wave now

You may hear him at a rally
At a march on the front lines
Or even catch his first book *Imaginary Borders*
Where he writes, "the future is as much yours as it is mine."
With long hair, he moves, he dances, he sings
He kicks a rhyme
Xiuhtezcatl

Lights out.

SCENE 7
FOOOOOD
Written by Karla Jackson-Brewer

An image of Frances Pérez-Rodríguez along with her name is projected on a screen prior to the poem.

Lights up.

KARLA:

1790
Black hands in West African dirt
Sustain the village with
Millet and cassava
Staples for a genetically healthy diet.

Stolen Black hands in Louisiana clay
Harvesting sugar cane for a European sweet tooth
Cane juice mixed with blood and sweat
Sweets, food, bodies
Commodities, all.

Years pass, centuries,
Bring us to now when we no longer touch the soil
Separated by land and sea and agribusiness
Modified food, for modified bodies
We have lost our connection to what nourishes us.

1990
Our local purveyor of food and sundries
Crowded with neighbors filling carts with goods that can
Sustain them for the work week in a frenzied New York City.

The Eco Rise

Before the gentry arrived, there were limited selections
Of fruits and vegetables, often wilting on the shelves,
Peaches that never ripened into juicy sweetness,
Strawberries that had no taste.

Poorer communities were sold a poorer quality of food.
What can you do if that is all there is?

2006
An organic section begins to sprout
From the compost of bruised fruit and wilted vegetables,
Its roots have spread
Weaving itself like a vine throughout the store.
Organic produce blooms and blossoms
Separated from conventional produce
By bright signs and hefty prices.

When did kale become an exotic superfood?

Black folks have been eating kale and other greens for decades.
Alaga Syrup, a staple on many a table in the Black South,
On many a table that migrated North, increases in cost
Thanks to an organic label.
Rising prices from trendy marketing & popularity
Dissuade poorer families from eating a sustainable diet.
Diets rich in saturated fats, sugar, processed meat,
White bread, and starchy vegetables,
Fill the family table
Satisfying in the moment,
Wreaking havoc in the body over time.

When was the last time you put your hands in some soil?
Got the satisfaction of nurturing a seed to a sprout,

Poetic People Power

A sprout to a stem,
A stem to branches and leaves,
And flowers to fruit?
When last have you tasted and shared that
Magical goodness of your attention and love?
When last have you nurtured the ground that
Nurtures the plants that nurture your body?

1980
Community Gardens movement cultivated
Land reclamation
In abandoned New York City lots
Hands in the ground experience.
Growing CSAs for local underserved communities,
Immigrants, refugees & survivors of state violence,
Creating equitable access to healthy food
Advocating an anti-racist platform
Of the right for all to have agency in
The food system.
Freeing us from the dependence on agribusiness—
A revolution on the land.

2018
Women of color
Help us remember
   Our connection to the earth
      Our connection to the collective
         Our connection to our history and culture
           Our ability to sustain ourselves in urban and rural locations.

Urban harvester
Frances Pérez-Rodríguez,
Member of La Finca del Sur

The Eco Rise

1st Black & Latina-led urban community farm
Rising from the ashes of a burned-out South Bronx
Reclaiming that land to nourish and heal the community.
Staking the knowledge that grows in Caribbean, Mexican,
& Southern Black folks' memories.
Herbs that heal and stimulate the palate
Cultivated on an urban farm
Employing farming techniques which have historically
Sustained people who have left——home
To live in this glass and metal landscape.
Sprouting power and agency from young to old
The message—reject agribusiness. Eat your own harvest.

How does your garden grow?

Farmers' market conversations over
Heirloom tomatoes, simmer a commitment
To sustainable food systems and local food economies.
Like seeds blowing across fields,
Cross fertilizing a movement
That takes back the power of food.
Tilling the soil to resist climate change,
Weeding out the gentrification of food,
Re-seeding a revolution of agency and autonomy,
We feed ourselves!

Affirmation:
Grow your own meals
      Share your garden's bounty
            Sell to your neighbors

Poetic People Power

2023
What will we do when the sun shines so hot
Rivers are like hot tubs?
What will we do when:
The ground and air are so moist and humid
Palm trees sprout in cracks in the sidewalks?
Yellow and dengue fevers are as common as the flu?
Mold covers buildings like ivy?
What will we do when spring does not come
Till the swelter of June?
What will we do when the food we eat
No longer arrives in the truck?

We follow the lead of
Frances, and
Others like her around the world.
We put our hands in the earth
  We seed our flower boxes
    We sustain ourselves
      With our
        Home
          Grown
            Food.

Lights out.

SCENE 8
Earth's Lawyer
Written by Tara Bracco

An image of Polly Higgins along with her name is projected on a screen prior to the poem.

Lights up.

(Voiceover of imagined dialogue.)
ERICA: 911, what's your emergency?
BOGAR: She can't breathe. She's choking.
SUZEN: Oh my god. Please help. She's been poisoned.
PHILIPPE: Come quick. There's been a stabbing. She's hurt badly.

(Beat.)

TARA:

There's an emergency happening
right now,
in our communities,
like a dark cloud
that brings a thunderous storm.
Do you hear the roar?
The desperate calls?
The pleas for help?

The voices are different these days,
louder, stronger, and quicker.
The fear is greater,

collapsing in on itself
like a forest of trees whose roots have died,
whose trunks have toppled over.

The language has shifted
from *change* to *crisis* to *emergency*,
to reflect urgency,
but there's no hotline
to call for this kind of crime.

When Mother Earth is
choked by pollution,
poisoned by pesticides,
stabbed by fracking,
where is the EMS and response team for this?
There is no nurse to breathe new air into her lungs.
There is no surgeon to restart her heart that pumps water
through her vein-like rivers.

When heads of states
allow our lands to be destroyed,
when industry contaminates our water,
when executives fund atrocities that devastate our neighborhoods,
who is held responsible for the harm done?

Harm done to:

Our land
Our water
Our communities

(Beat.)

The Eco Rise

We call her Mother

because her very existence supplies us with life,
the way a baby feeds off the breast of its Mama,
we live off her,

Mother Earth.

But she is being
strangled,
lethally injected,
assaulted.

She is dying.
Where is the justice?
Who will be held accountable?
Who will save her?

(Beat.)

Polly Higgins.
A London barrister
with a heart of hope, wide as the oceans,
looked out her window and had this realization:
"The Earth is in need of a good lawyer."

How, she wondered, *can we legally protect and defend Mother Nature?*

This question moved Higgins to action.
Leaving a well-paying job,
she set out on an important mission:
to hold perpetrators liable for
the crime of ecocide.

E-C-O-C-I-D-E

Extensive damage and destruction of ecosystems
must be made a crime.

Add ecocide, she demanded, *to the International Criminal Court
the way we have laws for war crimes and genocide.*

Abuses of this scale are too large not to be tried.
They ripple through communities, eroding land and spirit,
killing all that grows green and tall.

As resources are depleted to reap profits
and money rains down rich,
business, in this sense, is violence,
brutality against our Mother.

With no voice of her own,
her tears have turned from rain to too-frequent hurricanes,
her rage can be heard in volcanic eruptions,
and with each new unnatural disaster
she screams in distress to remind us:

We cannot survive without her.

Higgins stepped up to be her voice,
to say,
  Eradicate ecocide!
    Prohibit it!
      Preempt it!
        Prosecute it!

The Eco Rise

CEOs, governmental leaders,
must be held responsible for decisions that affect millions,
must be brought from ministry offices and boardrooms
into courtrooms.

She pleaded her case to the public and officials
in speeches, in books, in meetings, and in hallways.
Criminalize the abuse, she advocated.

Before Mother Earth bleeds out.
Before millions of lives are destroyed.
Before the destruction gives way to extreme devastation
that can't be undone.
Eradicate ecocide!

Our land
Our water
Our communities

Our life

(Beat.)

Higgins worked tirelessly for this cause,
until cancer took her suddenly,
poisoning her from the inside out
as if she was not just the Earth's defender
but the Earth's absorber.
Soaking up toxins like a sponge,
her body became a metaphor,
the inner contaminations eating away all
that is healthy and alive and beautiful.

Poetic People Power

If her life's work was a call to action,
her last breath was a foreshadowing of the decay to come.

Calling all climate protectors and conscientious objectors
from the Amazon to the Arctic!
Honor her passing, see her vision through.
The time is now.
Mother Earth is under attack.
We must trek forward on this path
Higgins began for us,
journeying through the jungle of the legal system
and venturing up the treacherous mountain climb to Justice.

So that soon, we can instead have this:

(Voiceover of imagined dialogue.)
ERICA: 911, what's your emergency?
BOGAR: She can't breathe. She's choking.
SUZEN: Oh my god. Please help. She's been poisoned.
PHILIPPE: Come quick. There's been a stabbing. She's hurt badly.
ERICA: What's your location?
           Help is on the way!

Lights out.

SCENE 9
EcoRise
Written by Tara Bracco

Lights up on poets.

BOGAR:
Kimberly Wasserman

SHETAL:
Pablo Solón Romero

SUZEN:
Peggy Shepard

PHILIPPE:
Sebastião Salgado

NABIL:
Xiuhtezcatl Martinez

KARLA:
Frances Pérez-Rodríguez

TARA:
Polly Higgins

They met the challenge
They did the work
They led the way for all of us
They did not give up
So channel your eco anxiety to eco activity

SHETAL:
Activate your resistance

KARLA:
Grow your garden

SUZEN:
Fight environmental racism

PHILIPPE:
Plant a forest

BOGER:
Change your community

NABIL:
Vote for the Earth

TARA:
Begin a new movement

BOGAR:
And know that there is power in numbers
And that power starts from within us

KARLA:
You are not alone
These stories we shared stand before you

SUZEN:
As information
As inspiration

NABIL:
As confirmation
That we can get on a better path

PHILIPPE:
A path to a planet where more things bloom than die
Where more things live than disappear
Where all life forms can not only survive but thrive
Where we dedicate ourselves to the eco rise

SHETAL:
The rise of eco consciousness
The rise of eco-friendly living
The rise of eco leaders

BOGAR:
Whose faces look like our own

SUZEN:
Whose faces look like our own

PHILIPPE:
Whose faces look like our own

NABIL:
Whose faces look like our own

KARLA:
Whose faces look like our own

TARA:
Whose faces look like our own

SHETAL:
(Slow and definitive.)
Whose faces look like our own

Blackout.

END OF SHOW

Can You Hear Me Now?

Can You Hear Me Now?

— Production Note —

Can You Hear Me Now? was presented live via Zoom on August 23, 2020. Created and produced by Tara Bracco, this spoken word show honored women's voices to coincide with the celebration of the 100th anniversary of the 19th Amendment, granting women the right to vote.

Bringing feminist voices to the forefront, the show gave women a space to explore what it means to be heard in their personal lives and at a national level. The show features original poems written and presented by Suzen Baraka, Tara Bracco, Shanelle Gabriel, Karla Jackson-Brewer, Angela Kariotis, and Shetal Shah.

This show was commissioned by Susan Grabel and Stefany Benson in conjunction with the exhibition Don't Shut Up 2020 at Snug Harbor Cultural Center, a project made possible in part by a DCA Art Fund Grant from Staten Island Arts with public funding from the New York City Department of Cultural Affairs.

— Producer's Note —

Artists were commissioned to write personal, first-person poems in any style that acknowledged important women who have inspired them and helped paved the way to the rights we have today. Each poet was assigned a word to focus their piece. The words—Write, Speak, Sing, Advocate, Protest, Vote—reflect the ways in which women's voices are heard, from the writing room to the voting booth. Presented via Zoom during the COVID-19 pandemic, we decided to incorporate masks into the show, specifically masks featuring a red handprint across the mouth, the imagery used by activists to raise awareness of Missing and Murdered Indigenous Women. This was explained in the pre-show remarks to be clear we weren't co-opting the image for our own use.

The show is dedicated to the memory of Julia Miles, who founded Women's Project & Productions, the Off-Broadway company now named WP Theater. Julia was my mentor and working at the Women's Project in my mid 20s is where I learned how to produce shows. There would be no Poetic People Power without her. During my years working under Julia's leadership, I saw first-hand how important it was to give space to marginalized voices. Julia helped build the careers of countless women theater artists since the 1970s. So this show is dedicated to her because Julia heard us first.

— Performance Note —

The words at the top of each scene—Write, Speak, Sing, Advocate, Protest, Vote—are intended to be displayed on a screen at the beginning of each scene. In the Zoom show, since poets were performing from their own spaces, the poets spoke these words before their poems.

— Publication Note —

Suzen Baraka's poem "Vote 2020," which appears in scene seven, has been previously published in audiovideo form, in a slightly different arrangement titled VOTE, directed by Jami Ramberan. It appeared online in PBS's *American Portrait*. In 2020, the video was awarded a regional Emmy in the PSA category. It also appeared in *2020: The Year That Changed America*, an anthology by Kevin Powell.

SCENE 1
Can You Hear Me?
Written by Tara Bracco

Lights up on each poet as they speak their first line.

(Poets speak with masks on.)

SHETAL:
I'm Shetal. I am a filmmaker. Can you hear me?

KARLA:
I'm Karla. I am a teacher. Can you hear me?

TARA:
I'm Tara. I am a journalist. Can you hear me?

SHANELLE:
I'm Shanelle. I am a creative. Can you hear me?

SUZEN:
I'm Suzen. I am a lawyer. Can you hear me?

ANGELA:
I'm Angela. I am a mother. Can you hear me?

KARLA:
Can you hear me?

ALL
(Overlapping, three times.)
Can you hear me?
Can you hear me?
Can you hear me?

SHETAL:
What does it take to be heard?

Lights out.

SCENE 2
A Young Feminist's Journey
Written by Tara Bracco

The word "WRITE" is projected on a screen. Then, the following quote is projected.

> "A word after a word
> after a word is power."
> —Margaret Atwood

Lights up.

(Poet takes off mask.)

TARA:

As a kid
I filled pages of notebooks and journals
with song lyrics/poetry/daily struggles,
adolescent worries coupled with adult anxieties.

I'd wake up in the dark
in my yellow childhood bedroom
and scribble on pieces of paper,
hoping I could read my brilliance
the morning after.

I was desperate then,
desperate with feelings,
desperate to make sense of my world,
        to find the words,
             to be heard.

Poetic People Power

Writing was a solitary act
back then
and the act was healing
for the solitary I felt.
It would be years before I learned
that scribbled words could be joined together
to make sentences that
        make sense that
                make change.

Words had a special power,
I knew, if I could get the words just right,
I could be understood/seen/known.

This was years before I took feminist poems
on the road with me,
packed in a backpack,
my notebook my sole source of company,
traveling across the country
reading punk poems in cafes and bars
to strangers in Chicago/San Francisco/Seattle.

Before I settled back in New York City
working for Erica Jong
where I learned a woman could be a writer
not only a teacher.
That words didn't have to be feminine/nice/pretty.
That the pen could decide fearlessly
what a woman wanted to say,
and once on paper,
an amazing new reality:
                It had been said because I wrote it.

Can You Hear Me Now?

But I learned
in my 20s
writing is not equality.
There would be no room of my own to think clearly
even as I read Wo(o)lf—both Virginia and Naomi

But still, I typed out stories on computers
with cracked screens/broken keyboards
from my bed,
not even a chair of my own/a desk of my own.
And I wondered if cramped spaces led to cramped minds
and cramped creativity.
Low wages were cramping my style.
My writing stifled before its voice
could take its shape.

This was before I would understand
that as women writers
we don't need just one room.
We need many rooms/expansive spaces,
created by a community of women who make room for one another.
Who prop each other up
with commissions/in zine publications/on stages.
This was my biggest lesson.

I sang along as Ani sang:

> "*some guy designed this room*
> *i'm standing in*
> *another one built it*
> *with his own tools*
> *who says i like right angles*
> *these are not my laws*
> *these are not my rules*"

Poetic People Power

So, I looked to women creating different angles,
who played by different rules.
My mentor—Julia Miles—
made room for female playwrights,
moving their voices from basements to Off-Broadway.

And my influencers didn't just show up in real life,
they sat on bookshelves:
feminists Marilyn French, Susan Faludi, Gloria Steinem;
poets Dorothy Parker, June Jordan, Asha Bandele.

With pencil in hand,
I underlined *Writing a Woman's Life*
and Carolyn Heilburn's words:

> "*Power is the ability to take one's place in whatever discourse is essential to action and the right to have one's part matter.*"

Book after book followed,
and I would create my institution of learning
from my bedroom,
issuing myself a master's degree in feminism and poetry
because library cards are how people without money learn.

I took everything I had
watched/read
from the female figures that came before me
and I created Poetic People Power.
Our first show—*Women's Words About War*—in 2003
spoke out against the unjust invasion of Iraq,
aligned with the Poets Against the War movement.

More and more
political presentations followed,

and I started shows thinking about
Audre Lorde's words:

> "...*poetry is not a luxury. It is a vital necessity of our existence. It forms the quality of the light within which we predicate our hopes and dreams toward survival and change, first made into language, then into idea, then into more tangible action.*"

And I kept writing because "*poetry is not a luxury...*"
And I kept singing because "*who says i like right angles...*"
And I kept advocating because "*power is the ability to take one's place...*"
And I kept producing so poets had not one, not two,
but 18 years of stages and spaces
for their voices to speak truths that rang from rafters,
hung in the air, and lingered in the hearts of listeners
for days after,
settling into people's minds
and then shaping their actions.

      Poetry. People. Power.
          Art + Action = Change!

My writing these days is still trying to make sense of the world,
but it's no longer solitary.
It's no longer desperate.
It's created in good company,
built out of community
with other poets
who are creating their own scripts for how to live their lives,
who are challenging existing societal confines,
who are realizing their strongest skill besides
the creative crafting of words

Poetic People Power

is the power their writing has
once it is
     read,
          spoken,
               and
                    heard.

Lights out.

SCENE 3
SPEAK
Written by Shetal Shah

The word "SPEAK" is projected on a screen. Then, the following quote is projected.

> "I speak not for myself, but so those
> without a voice can be heard."
> —Malala Yousafzai

Lights up.

(Poet takes off mask.)

SHETAL:

(Begin slowly.)
Speak
How? Speak out? Speak up?
To speak freely, to speak as equals among a sea of mores and men.
To be remotely valued at all,
depends
on which way fate swayed in the sea breeze
to descend which girl on what shore.
A shore that allows her to grow up, ascend and thrive?
Or simply survive and hope her silence keeps her alive?

Though it's true that women everywhere have shared in the fight
for the right to vote or to utter a word,
and to also have their ideas, thoughts and emotions matter,
in my ancestral land—
the peninsula of India—

the battle cry still remains barely a whisper.
I will admit that female voices are getting louder there,
but I hesitate to say
that brings me joy.

For the roots of male domination
are not easily removed and
I have witnessed first-hand
the fatal price paid
when mighty masculine demands are not obeyed.

Speak! I speak.
Silence! I am silenced.

These harsh tones are everyday fare
where,
my Indian sisters—
conditioned to honor
the commands laid on them,
by not only the heavy hands of men,
but also by a culture shackled
steadfastly to its divine belief in bad karma—
intuitively get that every second is a threat.
Every moment a reminder
that there are no spaces,
no pores within which they can openly speak,
and secretly scream out at fate in anguish or anger or rage or despair.

The power dynamics they bear
dictate they lie on the dark, dank and dusty side of the gender dividing line.
Roles, responsibilities, rules,
keeping them at bay,

Can You Hear Me Now?

should they even remotely
consider owning the right to say...
anything?

So, I snatch away the puppet strings
from the hands of my culture and its men
and snip the women free
from the weighty mandates
to always comply,
from the warped responsibility
to endlessly satisfy.
I take 5, 10, 20, 60, a lifetime of seconds of silence to breathe in deep.
Then exhale away the ways
in which my sisters' bodies are literally razed—
bodies and mouths that didn't submit,
and so were tossed live into flames,
or set on fire in a pyre.
Treated like a fragment of burning trash,
and cast against the law of a land
inked in scrolls that freeze the possibility of progress over time,
forcing my Indian women to forever act like 1950s American children.

(Speed up tempo.)
Me, American born, a '70s babe,
I am shaped from the cloth of an ancient country of hushed women
relegated to their places.
I raise my hand in female solidarity across time and space
because even nowadays,
in my 'modern' state,
I am not supposed to be heard above the din of:
(Various American male accents.)
"little lady, here's what you need to do"
or, "don't fret, sweetie, I will vote *for* you."

Though, ironic to say,
the women in my family were never that way, so
though my Indian culture threatens violence and rape
if I act outside my station,
my foremothers bore their bare arms toiling and digging
the path upon which I step.
My great-grandmother, the business owner,
my grandmother, the teacher,
my mother, the doctor.
Fingers gnarled from laying the groundwork,
I am supported by their sturdy backs.

Backs that breathed sound in and out,
even when it wasn't allowed,
each one of their voices fortifying the next—
to own their own business,
to teach,
to cure people of their cancerous ills.
And so, I add my voice to the resounding chorus that resides
within me and carries me towards the eager feet of my daughter
who will stand on me and SHRIEK.

The fallout from this steely strength lives inside me too.
Toughness and not letting too much love get through,
afraid that someone will swoop in and control me.
Will clamp my lips with their clothespin fingertips
so tight it pinches my skin.
I guess my culture, to some degree, still chokes me.

Speak. I speak. Silence. I am silenced, but only by the *awe* and *potential* of my
FEMININE power.
In reverence to the bare feet in whose imprints I tread,

Can You Hear Me Now?

I am determined in my promise to live up to their best hopes for me
that I NOT curtail my identity
at the hands of a society
that fears the escape of a woman's boundless capacity.

Instead we
realize our greatest power
lies not in toeing the line for the mainstream status quo
but in taking the more dangerous and costly route—
the simplest act of
opening our mouths.
Speak!!

Lights out.

SCENE 4
I SING
Written by Shanelle Gabriel

The word "SING" is projected on a screen. Then, the following quote is projected.

> "We were carrying the message of the movement through our songs."
> —Jamila Jones

Lights up.

(Poet takes off mask.)

SHANELLE:

I was born with blue lips
My cry was shrill but soft
My lungs
Like my mother
Needed assistance to keep me alive
I wasn't a child that would cry often
I found joy in existing
My stepmother taught me to open my mouth
Let words tumble out of my throat
Call praise to my lips
But only to improve upon silence
She never told me what to say
Something in me knew to sing
Something in me knew a melody
Could connect me to something greater than myself
My spine loved basslines

Can You Hear Me Now?

Tongue loved hymns
How lyrics danced and floated to echo on church walls
The organ vibrated from my frilly white socks
To the lace ribbons in my hair
I preferred singing to prayer
Varied keys locked and connected to the divine
Every time
The music transposed to a higher note
It's like my soul would float to the gates of glory
The choir was the only place for
Harmonies I heard in my head
The fermatas were cushions
Where angels would find a seat
When I sang
I knew there was a power there
Imagined the Mahalia Jackson in my blood felt it
I sing of her
Who sang aware of the
Force needed to unwrap the hate from the windpipes
Of Blacks at the Bible belt
I sing
Of *Strange Fruit* from an alto carnation
A depressed piano lagging behind Miss Holiday
Whose voice painted a hill of lynching
In a studio session for which her label refused to pay
Illustrated the stifling of a nation
Put its ugly on display for all to see…
I mean…hear
I sing of Josephine's spellcasting
With hips and feathers
High notes and
A fierceness that froze hearts
And forged fists

Poetic People Power

I sing of the light Jamila Jones
Gave to the room
With the additional verse
To the tune
We Shall Overcome

(*Singing.*)
"*We are not afraid*
We are not afraid
We are not afraid today
Oh deep in my heart
I do believe
We shall overcome someday"

That verse
That day in 1963
The police decided to speak to the song
Letting their guns be silent
See, it's in my blood to improve upon silence
To *Mississippi Goddam* at Carnegie Hall
Like Nina Simone
Cuss in a classy crescendo
In front of white folk in gowns and gloves
Who only expect me to entertain
To crescent my smile
To be a warm cushion like the bosom of a mammy
To find gratitude for simply sharing air
To seal my voice in a seashell
They open and close at will
I sang of oppression
And they told me to sing adagio
That I should be okay with my freedom in slow tempo
That the phrase will end soon

Can You Hear Me Now?

That one day my voice will be heard
The applause will come
But in between each note I hear the hush
My womanhood
Compounded by
Their tone towards my skin tone
Made my fight for my right to my song
A two-fold battle
Black women weren't allowed to place ballots
For nearly 5 decades after the 19th Amendment's ink dried
They opposed my need for forte
Because they know my voice can
Crush comfort and convict the guilty
Can bring down kings and
Reveal that righteous robes
Sometimes cover up the most filthy
But they're going to hear me
They're going to hear me
And they can spill my blood
Till my body is empty
Till my career is over
Till they call me crazy
As if that's not the place they drove me
They can tarnish my legacy
But I need to
I'm going to
I have to sing
Till every voice is free to join me
Till every woman is seen and heard
Till every man can hear no
And there be no confusion
Till my input in this world is valued
Till my worth is no longer limited to

My ability to bear child or sit and smile
Till I see reflections of me in every government seat
Till my body belongs to me
Till every vote is counted
Till every machine in every Black county
Is not broken
Till women are given credit
For how they continuously make this world whole
I'm going to sing of hope
Create a song for every key
To be sung together
By every woman
A choir weaving harmonies
We will turn every place we stand
Into our tabernacle
The bassline be our heartbeat
Dreaming that one day each note
Will come closer to equality
And we will sing like Ida B. Wells
And we will sing like Hallie Quinn Brown
And we will sing like Frances Ellen Watkins Harper
We will sing
We will sing
Sing

(Singing.)
Oh deep in my heart
I do believe
We shall all be free someday

Lights out.

SCENE 5
Women at Work
Written by Angela Kariotis

The word "ADVOCATE" is projected on a screen. Then, the following quote is projected.

> "Each time a woman stands up for herself...
> she stands up for all women."
> —Maya Angelou

Lights up.

(Poet takes off mask.)

ANGELA:

Women do the ADVOCATING
They do the calling in and calling out
The calling UP
Women do the birthing and the dying
Women do the changing
The cleaning
The clearing
The sifting
The lifting
The shifting
The raising
Dream building is
     Women's work

Women do the mending
The careful stitching/back together
The making/this world fit right

Poetic People Power

Women measure twice and cut once
Wrap it up tight
Slice with a switchblade tongue
Pierce the air
Punctuate the point
Not earning a living, earned to live right
The women doing women's work

She, Angela Davis
She, Dolores Huerta
She, Patrisse Cullors
She, Ursula K. Le Guin
She, Wilma Mankiller
I
I
I
Calling through a bullhorn
Soothing in a whisper
Talking through a conch shell
She read the writing on the wall
You
You
You

Women do the won't stop, don't stop
Holding her to a different set of stakes and adjectives

HE is Confident
    SHE is arrogant
HE is Righteous
    SHE is angry
HE is Organized
    SHE is demanding

Can You Hear Me Now?

HE is Intuitive
    SHE is emotional
HE is Powerful
    SHE is too masculine
HE is Brave
    SHE is reckless

Her name was Joanna, in the 5th grade, who stepped to the bully, tore off his hat, threw it to the asphalt and screamed, "Hey! You can't do things like that!"

Do you have the audacity? Like her.
Do you have the temerity? Like her.
Will you put your foot down? Unwavering. Unmoved. Unflinching.
Rock/rock/rock/rocking steady? Like her.
Are you willing to scream, "Hey, you can't do things like that!"

The women's movement
Their moving
Runs to save our lives

Working an hour for the price of a coffee
Pumpkin spice and a cinnamon stick
Dragging yourself in, scared to call out sick
79% of the teachers are white and the majority of the students aren't
We don't want to defund police but have no problem defunding education
If you want to stop giving money to it, just rename it "the arts"
Working twice as hard for half the respect, a third of the pay
Not a penny for the thought
Switching policy at the turn of a dime
You can't even find the office for Title IX
Gabriel Fernandez's social workers won't do time

Poetic People Power

Dylann Roof got to walk away alive
Read the subtext in between that thin blue line

She was the one who threw the hat on the asphalt, the gauntlet, drew the line in the sand and proclaimed, "Hey, you can't do things like that!"

Doing women's work/everything on the line/waiting line/dotted line/ blood line/lifeline/voting line/picket line/lunch line/strike line/hotline. Chalk outline. Nameless. She calls us to the frontline. Get in formation!

In the name of the mother, and daughter, and her holiest of spirits

Malala
Malala
Malala

Brianna
Cara
Claudia

Lourdes
Felani
Ihsan

Evangelia
Panagiota
Photini
Joanna
Ave Maria
Maria
Maria

Can You Hear Me Now?

Glory be
#SayHerName
In her name. We pray.

Calling through a bullhorn
Soothing in a whisper
Talking through a conch shell
She read the writing on the wall
I
I
I
She, Hazel Scott
She, Kate Bornstein
She, Tarana Burke
She, Maya Lin
She, Dorothy Day
She, Dora Lee Jones
She, Fannie Lou Hamer
She, Jovita Idar
She, Yuri Kochiyama
She, Lucy Parsons

Find the light to be lit—ignite it
What's the law to be writ—write it
Find the voice to be lifted—sing it
Grab the hand to be held—hold it

Can you brave the storm? Like her.
Will you do your part to bend the arc of justice? Like her.
Is the room better with you in it? Like her.
YOU
YOU
YOU

Poetic People Power

Calling through a bullhorn
Soothing in a whisper
Talking through a conch shell
She read the writing on the wall

What are you afraid of?
SHE is what you're made of.

Lights out.

SCENE 6
PROTEST
Written by Karla Jackson-Brewer

The word "PROTEST" is projected on a screen. Then, the following quote is projected.

> "Get out in the street. Scream; sound alarms...
> We got to protest."
> —Ruby Dee

Lights up.

(Poet takes off mask.)

KARLA:

    I protest for humanity
    I protest anti-Blackness
    I protest state violence
    I protest for change

PROTEST
An action not in agreement with your plan
Resistance to the status quo
Going against the grain
A work slow down
I disagree
SHUT IT DOWN!

NO!
A simple
2 letter word
Spoken

At 2-years-old
Turns into a banshee's wail
NOOOOOOOOO!
          PURE POWER
At 7 months
You meet the boundary
My mouth clamps shut
Refusing that grayish glob on the spoon
Passing itself off as something nutritious.
At 3-years-old
You meet the power
Of my silent protest
I sit down
On the sidewalk
I will walk no more.

      PASSIVE/ACTIVE PROTEST

PROTEST is in my DNA
From the time my ancestors
Arrived on this land
They found ways to
Outwit oppression
IN PROTEST.

1776
She walks into the woods
At the edge of the plantation
Not allowed to leave the property
Body bound to that specific land.
Yet, there it is just across the road
Teasing her,
Right beyond her grasp,

Can You Hear Me Now?

She is compelled,
Driven by an urge
So primal and transgressive.
        SHE WILL RISK
Slave patrols and whip
To find it.
Emerald green leaves with ridges and patterns
Delicate bursting lilac flowers
Resting against green background
Fragrant and fresh
Pennyroyal
Good for a cold;
Good to bring on the blood flow
When it's stopped by an unwanted seed of Massa.
Sharing herbs and tea with others,
She chooses, hard choice!
No more life added, to
Increase the wealth of this Southern planter.
Massa ponders
"For over 2 years, no children born here."

(Sucking teeth sound.)
He think we stupid
        PENNYROYAL PROTEST
Undermines his wealth.

1878
At 16, Ida rails against
The splitting of her family when
Her parents die;
She becomes mother
Passing herself off as older
She works as a teacher

Poetic People Power

Required to teach a curriculum
Designed specifically for Blacks
That removed phrases like
"Liberty and freedom for all,"
An education filled with repressive lies.
Protesting the veiling of the truth
She is fired,
Freed,
She uses the written word,
Denied to her ancestors.

She uses the written word
to reveal what is only shared in whispers,
The cowardly mob violence happening
Deep in the night.
She uses the pen like a sword
Cutting shame across the faces of white patriarchs
Shaming an American president to
Take action against lynching.
She uses the pen
To remind Black people
That they don't have to accept
Living without dignity,
Being treated like dogs,
In cities like Memphis.
She uses the pen like a beacon
Beckoning Blacks to go West
And start anew as humans.
White elites never know the voice
Behind the pen
Threatening castration
To the person
Publicly critiquing their behavior,

Can You Hear Me Now?

Exposing their racist violence.
(Sucking teeth sound.)
They think we stupid

Never knew it was a Woman, who
        PENNED PROTEST
Blacks disappear by morning.

Wife
Mother
Editor
Activist
Agitator
Truth always
Truth spoken
Without apology.
Ida squares off with Susan B.
Suffragettes
Betray Black women
In an attempt to court
The "Southern Sisters."
Don't come to the demo, they say,
Or if you must, please walk in the rear.
Strategic failure.
No vote for women till 1920.

(Sucking teeth sound.)
They think we stupid
        IN PROTEST
We take our chances with our men.

1940
Ella Baker

Crisscrossing the South on speaking tours
That instill a sense of pride and resistance in Black people.
Remember who you are
Black women, remember you have power.
She uses her power to organize Civil Rights
Voters' rights
Protests that put human lives on the line
Put human lives in the path of state violence.

Just like now.

Ancestor Ella directly
And pointedly
Speaks her mind.
Expelled from SCLC.

Her deep resonant voice
Heard as a challenge
Bruising Black male preacher egos,
She doesn't defer to male authority.

Banished to the ranks of SNCC.
Comfortable with the impatient energy of youth
She supports their need to take action.
Life spent protesting
Oppression,
Discrimination,
And colonization.

"We who believe in freedom cannot rest."
Ella's words
Buoy us on
We demand our due, and

Can You Hear Me Now?

Fight the power
Stop traffic
Make noise
Make a better
Home,
Family,
City,
Country,
Society,
World.

MY SILENCE
   A PROTEST TO YOUR INCESSANT INTRUSION
MY SHADE
   A PROTEST TO YOUR CONTROL
MY SASS
   A PROTEST TO YOUR ARROGANCE
MY LIFE
   A PROTEST TO YOUR CONTINUED ATTEMPT
   TO SNUFF ME OUT
MY LOVE
   A PROTEST TO YOUR LACK OF HUMANITY
MY CREATIVITY
   A PROTEST TO YOUR DULLING OF THE SENSES
MY SURVIVAL
   A PROTEST TO YOUR ECONOMIC THEFT

(Sucking teeth sound louder.)
THEY THINK WE STUPID

MY VOICE WILL NO LONGER BE SILENT
    THINGS WILL NOT GO BACK TO NORMAL
        NO MORE!

Lights out.

Poetic People Power

SCENE 7
Vote 2020
Written by Suzen Baraka

The word "VOTE" is projected on a screen. Then, the following quote is projected.

> "Voting is the only way to ensure that our values and priorities are represented in the halls of power."
> —Michelle Obama

Lights up.

(Poet takes off mask.)

SUZEN:
My mother relies on me
to help her save her Korean BBQ restaurant in NJ.

She does not understand
that this country doesn't care
about either one of us, or our survival.

All she knows is that Shake Shack got $10 million
and how come she hasn't gotten anything yet.

I tell her what the SBA representative told me:
That we filled out the application too early,
just before quarantine when Asian businesses
were already struggling because of the virus.
They streamlined it since then,
and threw out our application without telling us.
There's nothing left for businesses like ours.

Can You Hear Me Now?

I can tell this does not reconcile
with the version of America she dreamt of
in a country where freedom must of felt foreign to her
the way freedom feels foreign to me,
the way simply breathing feels revolutionary
in a country that targets Black bodies,
the way at 36 years old, this Black body
is afraid to make more Black bodies,

Like Black bodies ain't the people I love,
Like Trayvon don't remind me of my nephews,
Like Sandra don't remind me of my sister,
Like George don't remind me of my daddy,
Like Elijah don't remind me of me—
an introvert and different and unbelievably fucking strong—

Like being Korean and Black
during coronavirus in Trump's America
don't make me want to burn it all down.

I've applied for the NJEDA, the PPP, the EIDL of the SBA,
and I'm looking for the words to say…
I don't know how to help you Mom,
I don't know how to help you Dad,
I don't know how to help Trayvon,
I don't know how to help Oscar Grant,
I don't know how to help Breonna, Dominique or Tony.

But here I am talking to y'all about voting because I know…
Moses is a Black woman,
Shirley is a boss,
Sojourner Truth is a verb,
and they been telling us what happens to a vote unused:
It becomes an American dreamer deferred.

Poetic People Power

Just ask Stacey Abrams.
Voting is the bare minimum.
Hell, listen to Jade Simmons.
You can lead a horse to Maxine Waters,
but you can't make him think.
Alicia Garza in the Black Futures Lab,
tryna bring y'all Black to the Ballot,
and back from the brink.

Here I am trying to get people to vote because I know,
that between 2012 and 2018,
over 1.4 million voter registrations were cancelled,
with 500,000 cancelled in a single night in July,
and that's just Georgia.

Here I am trying to get people to vote because I know,
that in 2017, 99 bills to limit access to the ballot
have been introduced in 31 of these here United States
and I'm looking for the words to say:
If our vote wasn't important,
why are they working so hard to take it away?

Vote
Because Flint Michigan. still. doesn't. have. clean. water.
Because over 5,460 children have been separated
from their parents at the border.
Because children are being tear gassed,
Because children are being tear gassed
during the pandemic of a respiratory disease,
Because children are being tear gassed
during the pandemic of a respiratory disease
for protesting the murder of a Black man
by a white police officer via asphyxiation.

Vote
Because the war on drugs
led to Black fathers being ripped from Black babies, slavery.
Because the war on drugs
led to Black bodies being stopped, being frisked,
like it don't matter if Blacks live.
Because the war on drugs
led to ONE in 13 Black Americans
losing their right to vote due to a felony conviction.
That was 2016, the same year as Trump's election.
I said ONE in 13 Black Americans without a vote,
the same year as Trump's election.

VOTE because you want to make facts, facts again.
VOTE because the first step to co-opting a system is engaging in it.
Just ask the FBI, the CIA, Justice Roberts and Brian Kemp.
VOTE because when you're standing in the voting booth
trying to decide between tweedledee and tweedledum,
you'll ask yourself why there isn't a better choice.
VOTE because when they try to dismantle our bodies from our breath…
We gotta use our voice.

Lights out.

SCENE 8
Can You Hear Me Now?
Written by Tara Bracco

The following quote is projected on a screen.

> "Real change, enduring change, happens one step at a time."
> —Ruth Bader Ginsburg

Lights up on all poets at once.

(All poets speak without masks.)

TARA:
To find your purpose, write from your heart.

SHETAL:
To be heard, speak your truth.

SHANELLE:
To join the chorus, sing loudly.

ANGELA:
To change your community, advocate for your vision.

KARLA:
To demand equality, protest injustice.

SUZEN:
To change the country, vote because your rights and your life depend on it.

TARA:
Be creative.

SHETAL:
Be honest.

SHANELLE:
Be loud.

ANGELA:
Be bold.

KARLA:
Be outspoken.

SUZEN:
Be a changemaker.

TARA:
I am a writer. Can you hear me now?

SHETAL, SHANELLE, ANGELA, KARLA, SUZEN:
(One after another.)
I hear you.

SHETAL:
I am a speaker. Can you hear me now?

SHANELLE, ANGELA, KARLA, SUZEN, TARA:
(One after another.)
I hear you.

Poetic People Power

SHANELLE:
I am a singer. Can you hear me now?

ANGELA, KARLA, SUZEN, TARA, SHETAL:
(One after another.)
I hear you.

ANGELA:
I am an advocate. Can you hear me now?

KARLA, SUZEN, TARA, SHETAL, SHANELLE:
(One after another.)
I hear you.

KARLA:
I am a protester. Can you hear me now?

SUZEN, TARA, SHETAL, SHANELLE, ANGELA:
(One after another.)
I hear you.

SUZEN:
I am a voter. Can you hear me now?

TARA, SHETAL, SHANELLE, ANGELA, KARLA:
(One after another.)
I hear you.

TARA:
Yes, we hear you.

ALL:
(Overlapping, three times.)
We hear you.
We hear you.
We hear you.

SHETAL:
(Strong and definitive.)
You have been heard.

Blackout.

END OF SHOW

While We Were Sleeping

While We Were Sleeping

— Content Warning —

This show explores subject material that may be disturbing or upsetting, including human rights abuses, sexual assault, physical harm, and violence. Please proceed with care.

— Production Note —

While We Were Sleeping is a poetic theater piece that was commissioned by the International Human Rights Art Festival, led by executive director Tom Block, and premiered at the Festival at Dixon Place in New York City on March 4, 2017. Created and produced by Tara Bracco, this spoken word show uses poetic storytelling to illuminate human rights abuses around the world. The show was directed by Ben Arredondo. Subsequent performances with modified staging were presented at the Nuyorican Poets Cafe on December 9, 2017, to coincide with Human Rights Day, and at Secret Loft in Manhattan on March 15, 2018.

The show includes work written and presented by Tara Bracco, Philippe Javier Garcesto, Karla Jackson-Brewer, Shane Michael Manieri, Shetal Shah, Natalia Vargas-Caba, and Kesav Wable. At the Secret Loft show, the scene by Shane Michael Manieri was read by poet Jim Buckmaster, with permission.

This show was made possible with support from Left Tilt Fund, Louise Davis, and Wende Jager-Hyman.

— Producer's Note —

This show marked the first time the group worked together to present a performance with stage direction. Previously, our spoken word shows were presented with a single microphone center stage where I acted as emcee, introducing each poet, and providing a narrative arc to the show to thread the pieces together. In this show, we didn't break the fourth wall. Instead, we used sound and light cues as scene transitions to set the tone and shift between artists. Music specific to the geographical region of each scene was used to transition from scene to scene; for example, African drumming was heard before a scene set in Africa, Cuban music before a scene set in Cuba, etc. The audio cues provided not just a theatrical element but also helped shift the audience emotionally from some of the heavy content presented in the show. This show prompted me to develop a structure that included group scenes, which we subsequently used in the two other shows in this anthology.

To bring this staged show together, poets were commissioned to write five-minute pieces, based on research, to poetically tell the story of a human rights abuse happening somewhere in the world. They were instructed to put a human face on the issue, but not to speak for the people they were writing about. They could include, though, their own commentary, thoughts, and experiences. We also considered this a group show, and poets were encouraged to include the other poets in their pieces, either as a chorus or through dialogue, representing imagined voices, which are indicated in stage directions (i.e., British accent). The goal was to present a show where audiences travel around the world to learn about human rights abuses happening in our time, including in developed countries.

This was a challenging assignment for the poets, even for our artists who are used to writing on commission, because we needed some specific guidelines for consistency purposes. I'm grateful to the artists for their flexibility during this process, taking the risk to try something new, showing up to rehearsals after their day jobs, and working together collaboratively in a way that was a producer's dream. And we couldn't have done it without Ben Arredondo's direction.

The International Human Right Arts Festival booked us for a prime Saturday evening timeslot, and we performed to a packed house and received a standing ovation.

— Publication Note —

A version of Natalia Vargas-Caba's poem, "Oyeme Aqui," in scene three was previously published in *No, Dear*, issue 19.

Shane Michael Manieri's poem, "The Danger Isn't Over," in scene four is a found poem. The research documents can be found in the notes at the back of the book.

— In Memoriam —

The story of activist Anne-Marie Buhoro, who spoke out against the rapes of women and girls in the Democratic Republic of the Congo, is included in poet Karla Jackson-Brewer's piece, which was written in 2017. In January 2022, Buhoro was murdered. The Panzi Foundation states, "Her murder represents the risks that women take when fighting for change and raising their children in an environment where security is not guaranteed."

SCENE 1
Around the World
Written by Tara Bracco

Music transition.
Lights up. All poets on stage.

TARA:
Around the world today
There are injustices, violations, abuses
Of human rights
There are sadly
Too many names to name

PHILIPPE:
Too many tears to count

SHANE:
Too many
Gone too soon

NATALIA:
These are not the stories
Any of us want to know

SHETAL:
But to not look deep
Or to look the other way

KESAV:
When others are
Jailed

SHANE:
Beaten

KARLA:
Raped

TARA:
Sold

PHILIPPE:
Imprisoned

NATALIA:
Starved

SHETAL:
Killed

KESAV:
Is another form of violence
We must not be silent

KARLA:
So we read
And we look
And we listen

SHETAL:
And then we write
And we share what we know

Lights out.

SCENE 2
HOW
Written by Shetal Shah

Music transition.
Lights up.

KARLA:
(Indian accent.)
My daughter was very rebellious, disobedient...

TARA:
(British accent.)
My sister is 16 who says she'll be a solicitor. She's too Western thinking. She needs to marry or be shot and thrown in the sea.

SHETAL:
How
How can you
How can you raise these girls
How can you raise these girls in England and infuse them with life
How can you raise these girls in England and feed them, clothe them, bathe them, hug them, and kiss them night after night
How can you raise these girls in England
to believe in their own hope and promise
How can you raise these girls and neglect their desires
for the ways of the West
How can you raise these girls in a sealed cultural environment
As if they live on the same street in the same country that you knew
Theirs is a brand-new first-generation world view
It sparkles wide just past your front door
Inevitably, their bicultural worlds are not yours

KARLA:
(Indian accent.)
I warned her since age of 12 to behave and obey or else she will be killed for bringing shame to our family.

NATALIA:
(British accent, voice of teen girl.)
I go out after school and wear the latest trends. Amma and Papa are always on my back. It's just a pair of pants. And I think they look cool. I want to fit in, my friends wear them too.

SHETAL:
Your world…
Your world of social standing and family honor
Your world of shame and respect
Your world feels too tight, like a boa around her neck
That's why Shafilea put on lip gloss
and made friends with outsiders beyond Great Sankey
That's why Banaz ran away from that old, wife-beating man
you forced her to marry

NATALIA:
(British accent, voice of older woman.)
When I ran away from my husband, my parents threatened to kill me if I didn't go back. They see it as a big dishonor, like I've slated the family name.

TARA:
(British accent.)
People are talking bad about her, saying she stands too close to the boys. I told Ma to teach her a lesson.

SHETAL:
Couldn't you see the conundrum you put her in
Forced to conform to foreign rites of passage
Created in a land that echoes vaguely in her head
Reminded every day where the deed to her body parts lies
Under your mattress where you also hide
The key to the shackles around her sex
Ignorant that your daughter lives in two worlds—
the East and the West
They meet in the middle inside her breast—
the same one you co-opted then sold to just the right bidder
Not knowing that secretly she had a crush on her British babysitter

NATALIA:
(British accent, voice of older woman.)
When my husband raped me, it was like I was his shoe that he could wear whenever he wanted to. I didn't know if this was normal in my culture, or here. I was 17.

KARLA:
(Indian accent.)
My family and I are the victims of her behavior. Our honor needed to be mended. Why should we have to pay for what she did? Yes, of course it's her life I ended.

(Natalia steps behind Karla so she is no longer visible to the audience.)

SHETAL:
Yes, of course you did it because neighbors claimed it her fault
That she lured Uncle to open her virgin vault
And then refused when you demanded she marry his son
Yes, of course you did it because she commanded her dowry pay
for her books and her brain

And because she drives her own car and walks home alone
wearing high heels in the rain

KARLA:
(Indian accent.)
How dare she deny, deny, deny the privileges we place at her
feet. Our dishonor be damned, we'll rid of our shame come hell
or high waters. And marry off our three remaining daughters.

SHETAL:
Evil Eye was watching, the whole town knows she got soiled
And that made your motherly blood boil.
When the time came, family gathered to pre-meditate her fate—
The method of her obsolescence, to what hands-on torture
she'll be subjected—
Because unlike ordinary domestic violence
Honor killing needs multiple community members to perpetrate.
After some deliberation it was decided.
For Banaz, justice meant strangling by shoelace.
For Shafilea, the build-up to death was greater,
Suffocated with a plastic bag, dismembered then packed
in a suitcase thrown into the Kent River.
She and her femur showed up months later.
And the uncles and cousins egging you on in glee?
Ma, they praised you at best or simply shrugged and left.
You solved your problem,
The rumor mill has shuffled off to someone else's South London door.
Usually loud where you live
It hushes when asked by police,
No-one knows what happened,
NO-ONE makes a peep.
You saved your family's honor,
She'll never be seen again.

Finally, now, you can sigh in relief.
You know with certainty on whom you can depend
Because neither your dead daughter, nor your culture, will ever speak.

How could you raise these girls for 9 months in your womb
Then stab them 13 times when they wouldn't submit
to your do-as-I-say and say-as-I-do rules
How can you let simpleton talk fuel your mother hands to murder
How can you so readily remedy rumored shame and dishonor
How do you know those unsavory labels are true
After all, you forced her to obey you and only you
How could you raise these girls and then cut off their heads
with her brother at your side
How could you raise these girls, slash their throats and then burn them alive
How could you raise these girls then deny their gorgeous potential
How could you raise these girls
How could you
How

Lights out.

SCENE 3
Oyeme Aqui
Written by Natalia Vargas-Caba

Music transition.
Lights up.

ALL:
(Chaotic and overlapping.)
No Hay Comida.
There's No Food.

NATALIA:
Oyeme world, listen to me, my hand shakes to reveal
that in Venezuela a stretch of people standing
on Caracas asphalt wait eight hours or more to buy
meat and milk and flour—the supermarket shelves
are always barren. Take anything you can find: meat, milk,
and flour to make arepas, how they cling to traditions
under Nicolás Maduro's socialist empire—the people are
hungry, they march on the hot, melting streets to fill
dry shelves with pride for Venezuela, let them nourish
their bodies to overthrow Maduro. With every purchase,
Maduro records their fingerprints: if you bought meat and milk
and flour last week, you can't have them until next week.
Maduro says he can't promise them food. Maduro says
Obama stole their food. Maduro says they can wait for days
and leave with nothing.

Presidente Nicolas Maduro uses excessive force on Caracas
protestors who need more food: they are teachers, scientists,
architects, and nurses watching food prices fluctuate and rise—
milk and meat and flour require bags of bolívars to purchase,

the useless bills pile closer to God, though none have seen him—
The National Guard jailed one, José Salvador, did not let him
speak, they held him for a night in prison, beat and spilled his
blood, a red shadow, over a dark and creeping place.

Maduro is the successor to Hugo Chavez, socialist savior,
bought his wealth with oil reserves, yet did not invest
in the people. Chavez died in March 2013, Maduro
rose and took his throne. Socialism, for the people,
does not impose limits—here they are equals, they look
for food in dumpster bags. But behind supermarkets,
government directors load and carry carts of food.
Maduro keeps the government loyal with fruits and
fresh rice before the people's dusty hands take them.

The opposition banded to repeal the election—Maduro
won again—The opposition calls for a referendum, voter
fraud, yet Maduro stays in office. He recalled the one
hundred bolívar note, blames the United States
for economic instability, claims, to his citizens,
an "economic war" is unfolding.

Oye, Maduro shut off electricity four hours out of the day,
tropic heat rose and sank into their pores; people with dry
voices wear shirts that repeat

ALL:
(Together in chorus.)
No Hay Comida

NATALIA:
work hours tightened to two days a week; Caracas burns with tear gas
sprayed by the National Guard; no one walks out at night;

their bones crack, yet medicine hovers at high inflation;
Caracas police break their bones; guns are prohibited,
yet hunger drives the people to crime; guns are collected
under the black market; Caracas is the most dangerous city
in the world; murder rate at 120 per 100,000.

ALL:
(Together, loud to soft.)
No Hay Comida, No Hay Comida, No Hay Comida.

NATALIA:
Oyeme world, I know you do not hear of them much. Maduro quiets the journalists. Photographs of protests are prohibited. I write this to preserve those whose hunger swallowed them, who've died under the police's strangle: to Alejandro, Luis Felipe, José Salvador. Oye, if you do not hear of them again, listen to me speak to *Jesucristo* for their patria Venezuela and her children:

(All poets' hands in prayer, heads down.)
Padre nuestro en el cielo, librenos de nuestros pecados.

ALL:
(Praying.)
Father in Heaven, free us from our sins.

Lights out.

SCENE 4
The Danger Isn't Over
Written by Shane Michael Manieri

Music transition.
Lights up.

SHETAL:
The word Kuchu is a Swahili word for homosexuals. In Uganda, homosexuality is illegal, with laws dating back to the British colonial period.

PHILIPPE:
"If we keep on hiding, they will say we are not here… but of late, we are here."
—David Kato Kisule

SHANE:
Call Me Kuchu

David Kato, Uganda's first openly gay man,
born to the Kisule clan.
The younger of twins,

The founding member of Sexual Minorities Uganda,
assaulted in his home,
bludgeoned in the head with a hammer.

After his funeral, hundreds
of rainbow-colored balloons
were released into the sky.

While We Were Sleeping

Why is this a very strange thing to happen
in the middle of the day? Why
the beatings? Why the scars?
Why

The silence.
The endangered.
The stigmatized.

It's so painful it hurts.
And then there's the blood.
Blood,

coming from every part.
The Christian man walks
the streets yelling

Out with the homos.
Hang them.
Kill the Gays.

Homosexuals are a curse to the world.

Uganda is the result of hatred planted by U.S. evangelicals

who held rallies,
raided schools,
recruited children.

Calling for the hanging of
Screaming, *the gay movement is an evil institution,*

Forget about human rights.
Get used to your prison.

The human race will say we are not here.

ALL:
But we are here.

(Pause.)
SHANE:
The most dangerous terrorist isn't Islam
but one of God's names

is the avenger of blood
God loves Uganda.

God, love Uganda.
Have you worshiped that God yet?

(Beat.)

SHETAL:
A Luta Continua is a Portuguese phrase meaning The Fight Continues; it comes from the workers struggle in Mozambique and it was then borrowed by the LGBTQ struggle in South Africa. *A Luta Continua.*

The Fight Continues.

PHILIPPE:
A Ghost in the Guava Grove

SHANE:
Take a walk through the guava groves.
Smell the scent of the Barbie pink

blossoms. Listen
to the heroes that will never be.

While We Were Sleeping

To the moon's marble teeth
clack clack clacking

in the daytime sky.
The sun sizzling

as it sinks. With every step
in the tremendous grove

the garden stole
a wondering look

and, the killing flowers—
like the white winters of North America—

begins to shout, *Carnal. Carnal.*
Against the order of nature.

And suddenly the ghost of David Kato
rises from the ground

singing, "I want to be a good man not a dead one."

The danger isn't over.

(Singing.)
It's deep and dark and far far right.
A Luta Continua.

ALL:
(Singing in the same delivery as Shane.)
A Luta Continua

Lights out.

Poetic People Power

SCENE 5
War on Women's Bodies
Written by Karla Jackson-Brewer

Music transition.
Lights up.

NATALIA:
(Whispering, voice of a young girl.)
"Tell how we were taken from our house without knowing...tell how we were destroyed."

KARLA:
"Tell how we were taken from our house without knowing... tell how we were destroyed." Words 9-year-old Claudine, tells a reporter in the Congo—not her real name. But we must protect her now, because she wasn't protected that night.

In the Democratic Republic of the Congo, DRC, patriarchal objectification takes the form of approximately 2 million women and girls being kidnapped and gang raped.

Anne-Marie, Denise, and Claudine have suffered the ravages of war. They ARE the terrain upon which war is being fought, a war against all women.

Repeatedly kidnapped, gang raped, impregnated, and terrorized. Their flesh is torn to shreds, by a salvo used to assuage the defeated egos of male soldiers. Soldiers in search of a magical bullet-repelling potion, believed to exist in the inner recesses of young girls' bodies—gang raped for the blood of virgins.

Afraid, these girls are locked in a prison of silence and shame.

SHETAL:
(Congolese woman.)
When will this war STOP? WHO will stop this war?

KARLA:
Blinded by corruption the government is impotent. Slow to arrest, slower to convict.

PHILIPPE:
(Strong male Congolese voice.)
WOMAN BE SILENT.

KARLA:
Funds that might be used to medically repair, psychologically heal, and restore some semblance of humanity to these mothers, daughters, sisters, aunties, never arrives.

SHETAL:
(Congolese woman.)
Who will insure their health, their reproductive health? Isn't health a human right?

KARLA:
Kavumu village, DRC, 39 girls between the ages of 18 months to 11-years-old kidnapped and gang raped. 3-year-old Denise, not her real name, asleep one night perhaps dreaming of the things 3-year-olds dream of: playing in the village, singing a song, feeling the sun on her face... she sleeps in the quiet stillness of the night. Anesthetized by a substance that is blown throughout her village, she is taken, and raped by numerous men. Her mother wakes from an anesthetic stupor to find her child missing from the bed

they share. The village searches. Denise is found in a field, with rotting vegetation. Refuse cast aside.

She is a fortunate because she is taken to Panzi Hospital in Bukavu, where she sits shell-shocked on a bed, bleeding from the damage. No dreams of skipping in the sun for her. The tearing apart of the internal organs—bladder, colon, intestines, cervix, uterus, vagina—damaged by the human bombs that entered their bodies.

So young to have survived a night of hell; too young to live a lifetime with this horror. Fistulas formed from the tearing of the wall between bladder, vagina, or colon, allow fecal matter, menstrual blood and urine to leak. The constant odor is repulsive, an ever-present sign of the violence they endured.

Stolen childhood, stolen reproductive years, stolen by night terrors of brutal, senseless acts. Viewed as pariahs, these women and girls are rejected, further isolated from family and community.

November 2012, in the town of Minova, DRC, Anne-Marie Buhoro, a grown woman, was also raped in the night, as were 1,000 of her sister villagers. Courageously in December 2013, she revealed her identity during the governmental military trial. SHE testified against those who had been arrested. For eight days, 56 other women, covered in hoods to protect their identities, publicly told their stories, shared their shame.

Enduring threats that their throats would be slit if they continue.

PHILIPPE:
(Menacing male Congolese voice.)
WOMAN BE SILENT!

KARLA:
THEY did not keep silent.

THEY demanded Justice.

But Justice was not served—only 2 low level officers of 39 arrested were convicted of lesser crimes.

Hopes dashed, lives destroyed.

THEY and others keep telling their stories.

So all will hear & demand Justice.

Lights out.

SCENE 6
Jane Doe
Written by Tara Bracco

Music transition.
Lights up.

TARA:
I am a political artist.
I craft poems out of people's problems,
connect them back to policy issues,
and then give a call to action
for the change that must be on the horizon.

But there are some issues
even I didn't want to see.
So, when my friend Jonathan told me,
four years ago, that
I should produce a show about sex trafficking,
I turned him down,
not wanting to face the depths of these atrocities.

Then I learned at an event in Brooklyn,
that while I was sleeping,
the women standing before me were taken.
Their stories stayed with me for a year after.

> An educated mom from Asia trafficked right out of JFK airport after she gave her documents to a man she thought was from the employment agency.

> A twelve-year-old girl raised in the Bronx sold by a man she thought was her boyfriend until there were threats against her if she didn't do what she was told.

While We Were Sleeping

(Beat.)

So
I read news articles and watch TED Talks of women,
whose rights and bodies were stolen from them
just for

answering the wrong ad,
getting in the wrong car,
choosing the wrong guy.

And I re-learn a truth that I already know:
women are always vulnerable.
And the line between safety and danger is so thin
like the slice of the knife mark he left on her neck,
but the damage is long-lasting
like the crush of broken bones that ache
for years after.

The bruises on the bodies of women and girls who have been sold
are in various stages of color,
black/blue/purple/yellow.
But the psychological manipulation and the internal bruise of trauma
is much deeper and forever tender.

So, when I tell a survivor over coffee
that I want to share her story,
she says, *No.*
Don't re-exploit me.
There'll be no names here.
All these women, I'll call Jane Doe.

As I listen to their stories
I'm stunned by their bravery;

their ability to relive horrific details, publicly, through tears,
cause someone has to speak up, they say, *and prevent others
from being victims of crimes so heinous no person should ever
have to endure.*

In neighborhoods I visited for parties—
Williamsburg/Jackson Heights/Sunset Park—
women are forced against their will,
told to earn their way out,
and only once they've made their captor 30 grand
can they go free.

Make no mistake,
this isn't prostitution with agency.
This is an underground crime network
devoid of any humanity.

Women beaten with baseball bats,
drugged with white powder,
threatened with knives/guns/violence
into compliance,
moved daily
from place to place—

a brothel in Connecticut,
a bar in Queens,
and up and down I-95.

The moving of bodies in vans
as if they were products,
goods to be bought and sold,
men who treat women like dogs.
These buyers know, they must!
They can only enter with a code—

While We Were Sleeping

(A knocking sound.)
a certain number of knocks,
a series of doorbell rings,
a private phone number.

Only then are they let in,
where women are kept
locked inside,
like a prison
in small, dark rooms,
no access to a phone,
no washing in between
the relentless onslaught of men.

In fear,
their voices unheard.
Watched over.
Constantly controlled.

And as if being kidnapped, sold, and raped
ten times a day wasn't inhumane enough,
there are no meals given to them,
they're kept drugged, drunk, barely alive
on diets of pickles and rice.

And there's something that is said over and over
by survivors, counselors, and police officers:
    It could happen to anyone.

(Beat.)

Poetic People Power

(Tara steps left, speaks without poetic cadence.)
And then I remember. When I was eighteen, my sister and I traveled alone down to Miami. This was in 1993 after Hurricane Andrew. And we went down there to help rebuild houses for Habitat for Humanity. At the end of the week, we were the last ones left on the site where we were housed. And when it was time to go back to the airport, our ride never showed up. There we were, in this remote location, stranded, out of options, and out of quarters for the only pay phone when a man from a trailer down the way told us, he could take us. So, he went away and came back with a white, beat-up pickup truck that wasn't his, had 100,000 miles on it, and no gas. And we were running late and desperate, so we got in the truck and hoped for the best. When we finally arrived at the airport, we rushed up to the counter and told our story. The female ticket agent stopped her typing. She looked up. Her face stricken with concern, she said:

(Karla and Tara turn and face each other.)
KARLA:
"You could've been sold."

TARA:
(Tara steps right, speech returns to poetic cadence.)
So, here's what I know:
We cringe at our Southern history
where Black bodies were sold at auction,
but we deny a current reality—
right now
women are being sold in Brooklyn.
Stripped not only of their clothes,
but of their freedom, voices, and identity.
This is modern-day slavery.

While We Were Sleeping

And the words that stay with me the most
are the ones I want to reject
because they seem too unbelievable to be true
and yet,
I can't seem to get them out of my head.
> *It could happen to anyone.*

Lights out.

SCENE 7
Katarungan
Written by Philippe Javier Garcesto

Music transition.
Lights up.

PHILIPPE:
Ang bayan kong Pilipinas,
lupain ng ginto't bulaklak.
Pag-ibig ang sa kaniyáng palad,
nag-alay ng ganda't dilag.

(Translation.)
SHANE:
My country, the Philippines,
land of gold and flowers,
It was Love that, as per her fate,
Offered up beauty and splendor.

PHILIPPE:
At sa kaniyáng yumi at ganda,
dayuhan ay nahalina.
Bayan ko, binihag ka,
nasadlak sa dusa.

(Translation.)
SHANE:
And with her refinement and beauty,
the foreigner was enticed;
My country, you were made captive,
Mired in suffering.

While We Were Sleeping

PHILIPPE:
Ibon mang may layang lumpiad,
kulungin mo at umiiyak!
Bayan pa kayáng sakdal-dilag,
ang 'di magnasang makaalpas?

(Translation.)
SHANE:
Even the bird that is free to fly,
cage it and it cries!
What more for the country most splendid,
would she not yearn to break free?

PHILIPPE:
Pilipinas kong minumutya
pugad ng luhá ko't dalita,
aking adhika:
makita kang sakdal laya!

(Translation.)
SHANE:
Philippines, which I treasure,
Nest of my tears and suffering,
My aspiration:
to see you absolutely free!

(Beat.)

PHILIPPE:
It was the kind of rain that was incessant, melodious to the patter
   of puddles pleading
Halogen bit of brightness driving out the dark, though encroaching
   shadows always linger

Poetic People Power

Two masked men on motorcycle slay Romeo
Deflating the myth of Tigas, as he was known in the streets
Face down on the concrete, the police investigate, the flashbulbs
   capture a glimpse of raindrop
Washing away the blood spilt onto the Earth, another night, another
   extrajudicial killing
      Ang bayan kong pilipinas, lupain ng ginto't bulaklak

(Poet takes us back in time.)
The air is saturated with the smell of freshly fried breakfast
   longganisa, sinangag, at itlog
The heat bearing down so the people respond with umbrellas
   to cast a shade on themselves
Under the sun, Metro Manila's streets raucous with activity as cars,
   motorbikes, and jeepneys
Barrel down the streets charmingly by loosely following traffic
   lights and lanes
Young pre-pubescent street hustlers selling cigarettes in clapping
   wooden boxes
The masses are out in force for the inauguration of the 16th
   president of the Philippines
Rodrigo Duterte who swept the election with his hardline stance
   on drugs, corruption, and crime
The Davao man with a penchant for foul-mouthed tirades and
   misogyny has arrived at
Malacañang Palace, the symbol of ancient Spanish imperialism,
   rolled out the red carpet
As celebrities and elected officials proudly wear their barong tagalogs
Traditional embroidered shirts both sheer and white
If only such transparency was shown during governance
Integrity should be the cornerstone of civic duty
At a local rally on Mendiola Bridge marched thousands of
   activists who were in a surprising turn

While We Were Sleeping

Invited inside Malacañang to express all of their concerns
  directly to the president
Sowing the seeds though it is clear as crystal what they will
  come to reap
After the honeymoon period, after taking office as of
  June 30th, 2016, until January 30th, 2017,
7,076 deaths can be attributed to Duterte's war on drugs
Under Oplan Tokhang, the state's "Operation Knock and Plead" program
The accused are to acknowledge their guilt of pushing drugs or
  being a drug addict
And receive jail time, or alternatively may find themselves
Summarily executed by state-sponsored death squads, police
  and vigilantes
Who brand the accused with a cardboard sign around the neck
"Pusher Ako" or "I am a drug pusher"
Due process nonexistent

The war against Shabu or methamphetamines comes with
  overwhelming costs
Over 1.1 million suspected "drug personalities" forced to surrender
Sparking massive overcrowding of prisons
Quezon City's jail has converted the basketball court into
  a sleeping area
With inmates like sardines, a patchwork quilt of restless bodies
Sprawled, sitting, lying down, and considered lucky to have pillows

  Ibon mang may layang lumipad, kulungin mo at umiiyak!

I remember being 19, I received a call from my mother, she told me that my cousin had been robbed and murdered in Iloilo City. Shot in the gut with a shotgun blast while he was driving home from a party. They stole his wallet, cash, and cellphone. He was just 29 years young. Kuya Chris, we called him, the eldest of my cousins who took care of me when I was just a little gap-toothed kid. Took me out to the mall and we would play Nintendo or make-believe war games on the beach with an army of brats. Kid stuff. Shoot some hoops and eat hot dogs. He was taken from us: from his family, his wife, and son. The fantasy for revenge always lingers. It took eight years to convict and imprison his killers. The true victims are the families who survive, and though I cannot put a face to the families suffering, I know mine very well. Amplified by that feeling, in solidarity, I stand with them for justice.

> Pilipinas kong minumutya, pugad ng luhá ko't dalita

From the tragedy that befell my family upon the deeds of thieves and cutthroats
What is paid for in blood has fed the Grim Reaper, violence makes no distinction
Should Justice rain down with the ferocity of a thunderbolt?

These are criminals and addicts
Smite them like the Old Testament's wrathful patriarch
Self-proclaimed punishers, vigilante killers

But who will tell them when they've gone too far?
All in black with masks, riding in tandem
The driver and gunner, hit and run assassinations
Who gets to choose?
The tears of victims' loved ones swell into a tidal wave
Reconciled with rituals to help the dead pass over
Was paradise lost when we inherited the Earth or is our version of Eden still within our reach?
During his tenure as mayor of Davao, President Duterte bloodied his own hands

While We Were Sleeping

He admitted to the press that he killed three men
  suspected of kidnapping and rape
"I killed three of them, I don't know how many bullets
  of mine went into their bodies."

> *(Philippe and Shane singing together.)*
> Aking adhika; makita kang sakdal laya!

Lights out.

SCENE 8
El Sexto
Written by Kesav Wable
Intro and Outros by Tara Bracco

Music transition.
Lights up.

TARA:
Imagine
That I couldn't say these words
That my friends couldn't tell you these stories
That we were silenced, imprisoned for our art
For telling a truth a president doesn't want to hear
Imagine not being able to imagine
To create murals, sculptures, poetry shows
To create a new vision of the world we hope to live in

KESAV:
El Sexto, the Sixth
Danilo Maldonado Machado
Because, in 1998, habían five Cuban officers
incarcerated for espionage in America,
and dubbed heroes by Castro.

A persecuted voice in Castro's Cuba today
Danilo irreverently called himself the Sixth.
El Sexto. La voz del pueblo.
Machado refuses to be silenced in a land
where government terror snuffs, stifles
and suffocates the act of expression.

While We Were Sleeping

El Sexto, the Sixth. Danilo.
Te juro, speaking truth through art is his only crime.
Because you see, in Cuba, "artistic creation
is free, provided that its content is not contrary
to the Revolution." Article 39, Cuba's constitution.

Content not contrary to the Revolution?
Pero, eso es una farsa, verdad?
Because to create is to challenge, to subvert,
to imagine an alternative to the reality you're fed.
Tell a candle to burn in a vacuum. It can't.
Tell a political prisoner to rest peacefully on a bed.
He can't.

But the truth is, in Cuba, there are so many like Danilo,
thousands of political prisoners, prisons short on beds.
Dissident voices penned up behind cold concrete,
lie awake on dirty floors.
Like pigs penned up on the eve of their slaughter.
Content not contrary to the Revolution.

Never content. Never silent.
In 2014, he painted on two piglets the names "Fidel" and "Raúl"
and planned to release them in a park, where he envisioned onlookers
chasing and capturing los cerdos, as a prize; a nod to Orwell
and his *Animal Farm*. Only, his vision was cut short when authorities
arrested him before the performance even started, and jailed him
for 10 months; there, he was tortured physically and psychologically,
driven to a hunger strike, and even contemplated letting himself die.
No charges were filed and there was no trial.
Content not contrary.

Poetic People Power

The Sixth. Danilo Maldonado Machado of Camaguey.
He grew up poor during Cuba's Special Period,
when Soviet subsidies dried up, and left la gente
in despair. Arrested three times for his political views,
the most recent was in November 2016 for 55 days,
after he filmed himself spraying graffiti celebrating
the death of Fidel Castro. *Abajo Fidel, Abajo Raúl,*
he said into the camera on his phone.

Abducted, beaten and gagged, Danilo recounts in his sketchbook,
that he was transferred five times. The Sixth, in his sketchbook,
wrote a poem in Spanish, *The Sound of My Soul,* from within the walls
of a cell that could never contain his defiant, indefatigable spirit.
He wrote: "I want to know what I have done.
I want to know what is happening to humanity."
Content contrary to the Revolution.

Danilo, the Sixth, was released from prison on January 21, 2017.
But a creative soul like El Sexto knows this a false freedom, a sheen
designed to lull into complacence a lesser man, that for him is fleeting.
As long as his government uses arbitrary arrests and intimidation,
planting fear in its citizens,
violating their fundamental right to free expression,
Danilo Machado remains a soldier, speaking truth to authority.
¡Sigue El Sexto! Porque la libertad, Liberty—
If you want to reach it, and cannot wait,
Fear is an important thing to eliminate.

SHETAL:
Imagine with me the words that have yet
To form on your lips
Imagine art can live free and never has to be hidden

While We Were Sleeping

Imagine there are no limits to anyone's imagination
And may we all live in spaces that value
The craft of artists, the chants of protests, the strength of our voices
The differences of our otherness

Lights out.

SCENE 9
Rise Up
Written by Tara Bracco

Music transition.
Lights up.

All poets on stage, seated in chairs upstage.
Tara stands in the center.

TARA:
We write these words
And share these stories
Knowing that
While we were sleeping
Others were suffering
With so much taken from them
Abuses rise with every blind eye
And it's time now to turn
Information into compassion
Compassion into action
And action into a political and social justice movement
So loud and long lasting that no government
Man, woman, or community can ignore

As poets and activists
We want to live in a world where
Rights are inherent, not taken
Where bodies, hearts, and minds
Can't be broken
Where our rage over injustice
Leads to real change

TARA:
Around the world

(As each poet speaks their word below, they stand to join Tara in a line across the stage.)

KESAV:
Censorship

SHANE:
Homophobia

KARLA:
Sexual terrorism

TARA:
Sex trafficking

SHETAL:
Honor killings

PHILIPPE:
Government-sanctioned killings

NATALIA:
Governmental control

ALL:
(Together.)
Violating human rights

TARA:
With hopes of

Poetic People Power

(Poets each step forward on their words below.)
Freedom from slavery

KESAV:
Freedom of expression

SHANE:
Identity rights

SHETAL:
Gender equality

PHILIPPE:
The right to life

NATALIA:
The right to food

KARLA:
The right to our own bodies

ALL:
(Together.)
We dream and demand action

TARA:
In the names of

(Poets each step forward on their words below, moving from upstage to downstage.)
Jane Doe

SHANE:
David Kato

SHETAL:
Shafilea

KARLA:
Denise

NATALIA:
José

PHILIPPE:
Romeo

KESAV:
and Danilo Maldonado Machado

ALL:
(Together.)
We raise our voices

(Poets step forward as they speak with voices added to each line, until poets form a line downstage.)

PHILIPPE, KARLA:
We need to wake up

SHETAL, KESAV:
Step up

ALL:
(Together.)
Rise up

(Poets stand in a line.)
TARA:
From New York

KESAV:
To Cuba

KARLA:
From the Congo

NATALIA:
To Venezuela

PHILIPPE:
From the Philippines

SHETAL:
To England

SHANE:
To Uganda

ALL:
(Together.)
We bring
These stories
Centerstage

Blackout.

END OF SHOW

Notes

The notes that follow are intended to help clarify abbreviations used in scenes, to source material used in a found poem, and to source quotes in poems where it was not possible to cite the source within the work itself. These notes are included here at the end to not disrupt the flow of the reader's journey as they experience each scene within the narrative arc of the shows.

The Eco Rise

Scene 4, "We (must) Act" by Suzen Baraka

> MTA, Metropolitan Transportation Authority, https://new.mta.info/

Scene 5, "Tree of Life" by Philippe Javier Garcesto

> McKenzie Funk, "Sebastiáo Salgado Has Seen the Forest, Now He's Seeing the Trees," *Smithsonian Magazine*, October 2015, https://www.smithsonianmag.com/arts-culture/sebastiao-salgado-forest-trees-180956620/

Scene 7, "FOOOOOD" by Karla Jackson-Brewer

> CSAs, Community Supported Agriculture farms, https://www.ams.usda.gov/local-food-directories/csas

Notes

Scene 8, "Earth's Lawyer" by Tara Bracco

> Jonathan Watts, "Polly Higgins, lawyer who fought for recognition of 'ecocide,' dies aged 50," *Guardian*, April 22, 2019, https://www.theguardian.com/environment/2019/apr/22/polly-higgins-environmentalist-eradicating-ecocide-dies

Can You Hear Me Now?

Scene 2, "A Young Feminist's Journey" by Tara Bracco

> Margaret Atwood. *True Stories*. (New York: Simon and Schuster, 1981), 64.

> "I'm No Heroine", song by Ani DiFranco, from the album *Imperfectly*, 1992.

> Audre Lorde, *Sister Outsider: Essays and Speeches* (Crossing Press, 1984; 2007), 37.

Scene 3, "SPEAK" by Shetal Shah

> "Malala Yousafzai: 16th birthday speech at the United Nations," Malala Fund, July 12, 2013, https://malala.org/newsroom/malala-un-speech

Scene 4, "I SING" by Shanelle Gabriel

> "Jamila Jones oral history interview conducted by Joseph Mosnier in Atlanta, Georgia, 2011 April 27," Library of Congress, 11:35, https://www.loc.gov/item/2015669108/

Scene 5, "Women at Work" by Angela Kariotis

> Juston Jones, "When It Comes to Politics, Friendship Has Its Limits," *New York Times*, July 23, 2007, https://www.nytimes.com/2007/07/23/us/politics/23oprah.html

Notes

Scene 6, "PROTEST" by Karla Jackson-Brewer

Ossie Davis & Ruby Dee. *With Ossie & Ruby: In This Life Together.* (New York: Quill, William Morrow, 1998), 422–423.

SCLC, Southern Christian Leadership Conference, https://nationalsclc.org/

SNCC, Student Nonviolent Coordinating Committee, https://snccdigital.org/inside-sncc/the-story-of-sncc/

Scene 7, "Vote 2020" by Suzen Baraka

Darlene Superville, "Michelle Obama to headline voter registration rallies in Las Vegas and Miami," *Associated Press*, September 5, 2018, https://www.pbs.org/newshour/politics/michelle-obama-to-headline-voter-registration-rallies-in-las-vegas-and-miami

SBA, Small Business Administration, https://www.sba.gov/

NJEDA, New Jersey Economic Development Authority, https://www.njeda.gov/

PPP, Paycheck Protection Program, https://www.sba.gov/funding-programs/loans/covid-19-relief-options/paycheck-protection-program

EDIL, Economic Injury Disaster Loan, https://www.sba.gov/funding-programs/loans/covid-19-relief-options/eidl

Scene 8, "Can You Hear Me Now?" by Tara Bracco

RGB, Film by Betsy West and Julie Cohen (Storyville Films, 2018), 35:07. https://www.amazon.com/RBG-Ruth-Bader-Ginsburg/dp/B07CT8KKRZ

Notes

While We Were Sleeping

Scene 3, "Oyeme Aqui" by Natalia Vargas-Caba

Richard Washington, "Venezuela's Maduro turns to military in struggle to retain power," *CNBC*, July 15, 2016, https://www.cnbc.com/2016/07/15/venezuela-maduro-turns-to-military-in-struggle-to-retain-power.html

Scene 4, "The Danger Isn't Over" by Shane Michael Manieri

Nico Colombant, "Documentary looks into Uganda's Activist Gay Community," *VOA News*, March 2, 2012, https://www.voanews.com/a/documentary-looks-into-ugandas-activist-gay-community-141303483/180094.html

Jeffrey Gettleman, "Ugandan Who Spoke Up for Gays Is Beaten to Death," *New York Times*, January 27, 2011, https://www.nytimes.com/2011/01/28/world/africa/28uganda.html

Xan Rice, "Ugandan gay rights activist found murdered," *Guardian*, January 27, 2011, https://www.theguardian.com/world/2011/jan/27/ugandan-gay-rights-activist-murdered

Call Me Kuchu, film by Katherine Fairfax Wright and Malika Zouhali-Worall, https://callmekuchu.com/

"York Gay pride remembers Campaigner David Kato," *BBC News*, July 20, 2011, https://www.bbc.com/news/uk-england-south-yorkshire-14353703

The Legacy Project, "David Kato Kisule–Inductee," https://legacyprojectchicago.org/person/david-kato-kisule

Notes

"A luta continua," *Wikipedia*, https://en.wikipedia.org/wiki/A_luta_continua

"Call Me Kuchu," *Wikipedia*, https://en.wikipedia.org/wiki/Call_Me_Kuchu

"David Kato," *Wikipedia*, https://en.wikipedia.org/wiki/David_Kato

Scene 5, "War on Women's Bodies" by Karla Jackson-Brewer

Lauren Wolfe, "If 18-month-old girls are being gang-raped, why are the suspects still free?," *Guardian*, June 20, 2016, https://www.theguardian.com/commentisfree/2016/jun/20/girls-gang-raped-suspects-free-democratic-republic-congo-president-kabila

Scene 7, "Katarungan" by Philippe Javier Garcesto

Daniel Berehulak, "They Are Slaughtering Us Like Animals," *New York Times*, December 7, 2016, https://www.nytimes.com/interactive/2016/12/07/world/asia/rodrigo-duterte-philippines-drugs-killings.html?hp&action=click&pgtype=Homepage&clickSource=story-heading&module=photo-spot-region&region=top-news&WT.nav=top-news&_r=0

"Philippine Anti-Drug Operations Halted Over Police Scandal," *Associated Press*, January 30, 2017, https://www.nbcnews.com/news/world/philippine-anti-drug-operations-halted-over-police-scandal-n714141

"Philippines: Duterte confirms he personally killed three men," *BBC*, December 16, 2016, https://www.bbc.com/news/world-asia-38337746

"Abusive Philippine 'Drug War' Gets Military Reinforcements," *Human Rights Watch,* February 1, 2017, https://www.hrw.org/news/2017/02/01/abusive-philippine-drug-war-gets-military-reinforcements

"Bayan Ko," *Wikipedia,* https://en.wikipedia.org/wiki/Bayan_Ko

"Cardboard Justice," *Wikipedia,* https://en.wikipedia.org/wiki/Cardboard_Justice

Scene 8, "El Sexto" by Kesav Wable

"Cuba 1976 (rev. 2002)," *Constitute Project,* https://www.constituteproject.org/constitution/Cuba_2002?lang=en

Andrea Torres, "Cuban artist 'El Sexto' releases sketches from Havana prison," *Local 10 News,* December 20, 2016, https://www.local10.com/news/2016/12/20/cuban-artist-el-sexto-releases-sketches-from-havana-prison/

Contributors

BOGAR ALONSO is a mosaic writer and creator. His films have premiered at international film festivals, and his editorial and journalistic work has been published on *Vice*, *Gawker*, and *HuffPost*. He has also been a finalist for emerging artist competitions in the poetry and TV worlds. He is the writer and director of the film *Rodney*.

SUZEN BARAKA is an Emmy Award-winning poet, writer, actor, and activist. She began her acting career starring in *Everlasting*, recipient of the Viewer's Choice Award at the 2020 Cannes Short Film Festival. During the pandemic, she wrote, starred in, and released VOTE, originally commissioned by Poetic People Power, directed by Jami Ramberan, and published in Kevin Powell's anthology *2020: The Year That Changed America*. She appeared in *Let America Be America Again* produced by Creatives4Biden for Election Day 2020, and she's been featured at Ars Nova's #OATH2021 and at Restart Stages at Lincoln Center.

TARA BRACCO is the founder and producing artistic director of Poetic People Power. She has created, produced, and performed in 20 spoken word shows about social and political issues. She is a recognized leader in the field of art and social change and has been featured in *O, The Oprah Magazine*, *Time Out New York*, *Brooklyn Rail*, and *HuffPost*. She

137

has spoken about art and activism at colleges, festivals, and theaters, and she is the recipient of 20 competitive grant awards from funders including the Puffin Foundation, Left Tilt Fund, PEN America, and Lower Manhattan Cultural Council. Her work as a journalist has been published by *Cosmopolitan*, *American Theatre*, *Condé Nast Traveler*, *BUST,* and *Clamor*. She is also the recipient of the 2015 Images and Voices of Hope Award. In 2009, she cofounded the international nonprofit The Project Solution, which serves 30,000 people in 14 countries.

SHANELLE GABRIEL is an internationally touring artist, educator, and lupus warrior from Brooklyn, NY. Widely known for being featured on HBO's Def Poetry Jam, she has shared the stage with artists such as Jill Scott, Nas, Nikki Giovanni, and Talib Kweli, among others. In 2006–2007, she competed in the National and Individual World Poetry Slam Competitions. She has penned and been featured in global poetry campaigns with Pandora Music, LifeWtr, *Inc. Magazine*, Eden BodyWorks, and she has three albums fusing music and poetry. She is the executive director of Urban Word, an organization that founded the National Youth Poet Laureate Program and uses poetry and hip-hop to promote literacy and youth voice.

PHILIPPE JAVIER GARCESTO is a Filipino-American actor, mixed media performance artist, poet, martial artist, and karaoke enthusiast. He has a varied film and theater background, but he is most proud of the roles where he has been able to portray Filipino characters in media. Most recently, he starred in the award-winning comedic short film *Filipinos Get Some*. He graduated from Rutgers Mason Gross School of the Arts with a BFA in Visual Arts. He credits his martial arts practice for renewing his purpose towards pursuing his creative goals as an advocate for diverse stories and uplifting the global community.

Karla Jackson-Brewer is an educator, an optimist, an integrative therapist, and a teacher of numerous spiritual traditions. An activist for social change in the anti-violence movement, she has spoken out against racial, gender, and class inequality all her life. She has been published in *Ikon Magazine*, *Women of Power Magazine*, and *Skin Deep: Women Writing on Color, Culture and Identity*.

Angela Kariotis is an artist as public servant. She is a community-engaged culture worker and educator building creative experiences, serving the needs of cities, institutions, and students of all ages for public good. She integrates restorative practices with the pedagogy of play for a transformative learning experience. As a performance artist, her work has been presented by venues, including UCLA, University of Texas at Austin, People's Light, Legion Arts in Iowa, and Contact Theater in Manchester, UK. The arts education program she co-created and facilitates, Walking the Beat, was awarded a grant from the NJ Attorney General's Office as a Community Based Violence Intervention Program.

Shane Michael Manieri is a poet whose work has appeared in *Lambda Literary Review*, *Painted Bride Quarterly*, and *Vinyl Prose and Poetry*. He has taught writing at Columbia University and worked with ESL students in Brooklyn. He also helped create the Buddhist outreach group QueerDharma, which raised funds for the Ali Forney Center, an LGBTQ homeless shelter, and has volunteered as a Big Brother at the Incarnation Children's Centre. He holds an MFA from Columbia University, has received a full-immersion language grant from the Italian Cultural Institute, and is currently working on his PhD in comparative literature at CUNY Graduate Center.

SHETAL SHAH is a performance poet, award-winning actor, and Emmy award-winning filmmaker. She was an invited poet for Lincoln Center's La Casita Festival and has performed at the Nuyorican Poets Cafe, Bowery Poetry Club, and across New York City. Shetal's activism includes policy work on climate change and the Global South in collaboration with various NGOs, and the United Nations and its delegations. She is a graduate of Maggie Flanigan Studios and the LAByrinth Theater Master Class. Favorite acting credits include: *Acquittal* (Pan Asian Rep) and *Truth Be Told* (Ensemble Studio Theatre). Shetal's latest short film, *Off Duty*, is now distributed worldwide after winning awards at U.S. and international film festivals.

NATALIA VARGAS-CABA is a graduate of Sarah Lawrence College in Creative Writing and Spanish. Her work has been published in *No, Dear* and *Babbling of the Irrational*. She is a technical writer in her day job.

NABIL VIÑAS is a 2021 Cine Qua Non Lab Resident and 2019 NYSCA/NYFA Artist Fellow in Screenwriting from the New York Foundation for the Arts. An award-winning actor, his films have played festivals worldwide, including New York Film Festival at Lincoln Center and HBO's New York Latino Film Festival, and he's acted with theatre companies, including LAByrinth Theater and Cleveland Play House. Most recently, he co-created the play *Being Chaka* with TÉA Artistry (Archive Residency, New Ohio Theatre), and he's currently developing the feature film *Los Malos*. He is also a dedicated human rights advocate.

KESAV WABLE is an actor and writer best known for his award-winning play *For Flow*, which he developed as a fellow at the Lark Theatre. He later adapted the play into a short film, which was selected as a finalist at the 2011 HBO American Black Film Festival and subsequently aired on HBO/Cinemax. He is also an attorney who practices law in New York City.

Stay Active!

Each show program included resources and information for audience members to learn more about the issues presented. The following recommended websites appeared in the show programs.

The Eco Rise

Arts & Climate Initiative, artsandclimate.org

Inside Climate News, insideclimatenews.org

Climate Nexus, climatenexus.org

Earth Guardians, earthguardians.org

Earthjustice, earthjustice.org

Grist, grist.org

Little Village Environmental Justice Organization, lvejo.org

Stop Ecocide, stopecocide.earth

WE ACT, weact.org

Woke Foods, wokefoods.coop

Can You Hear Me Now?

Register to Vote, vote.gov

Rock the Vote, rockthevote.org

League of Women Voters, lwv.org

Stay Active!

Emily's List, emilyslist.org

National Organization for Women, now.org

National Women's Law Center, nwlc.org

Equality Now, equalitynow.org

American Civil Liberties Union, aclu.org

Black Lives Matter, blacklivesmatter.com

Native Women's Wilderness, nativewomenswilderness.org

Malala Fund, malala.org

A Room of Her Own Foundation, aroomofherownfoundation.org

Feminist Press, feministpress.org

Fuller Project, fullerproject.org

Women's eNews, womensenews.org

Ms. Magazine, msmagazine.com

Bitch Magazine, bitchmedia.org

WP Theater, wptheater.org

While We Were Sleeping

Amnesty International, amnesty.org

Human Rights Watch, hrw.org

UN Watch, unwatch.org

Equality Now, equalitynow.org

Karma Nirvana, karmanirvana.org.uk

Iran and Kurdish Women's Rights Organization, ikwro.org.uk

Sexual Minorities Uganda, smuginternational.org

Panzi Foundation, panzifoundation.org

Mentari, mentariusa.org

Stay Active!

Safe Horizon, safehorizon.org

Philippine Alliance of Human Rights Advocates, philippinehumanrights.org

Foundation for Human Rights in Cuba, fhrcuba.org

Acknowledgments

This book marks the first time in the project's 20-year history that any of the shows have been published. I'm incredibly grateful to Dr. Ross Tangedal at Cornerstone Press for seeing the value of our work and embracing this anthology. I've long led Poetic People Power, advocating for these artists, and with this book Cornerstone Press is making our work accessible to a larger audience. I'm also grateful to other staffers at the press including Brett Hill, Ellie Atkinson, Carolyn Czerwinski, Ava Willett, and Natalie Reiter.

This book also greatly benefited from the brilliant input of freelance editors Jennifer Gandin Le and Rebecca Kinzie Bastian. As I worked with the poets to edit their work, Rebecca worked with me to edit my own poems, and she helped capture the spirit of my pieces and strengthen my work on the page. Editing this anthology was a complex process, and Jennifer offered invaluable guidance by providing a path forward to edit this book, offering supportive advice, editing for consistency, and proofing my work. I couldn't have prepared this book for publication without her.

When I set out to publish a book, I received advice from Chantal Bilodeau, Jonathan Walton, Molly MacDermot, and Colin Robinson—all who kindly provided information and direction early in this process, before a publisher was identified. The Authors Guild and Ryan Fox Law were immensely helpful in providing knowledgeable and

Acknowledgments

necessary information about the business side of publishing, and I'm grateful for their expertise and commitment to writers.

As mentioned in the production notes, these shows were made possible with funding from the Puffin Foundation and commissions from Susan Grabel at Snug Harbor and the International Human Rights Art Festival. Also mentioned in the text before the shows are the acknowledgments of pieces that have been previously published elsewhere.

Over the years, more than 100 people helped make the Poetic People Power shows happen in New York City. This includes: people who volunteered to set up shows, work the box office, and hand out programs; professional photographers, videographers, and designers who worked for fees below market rate; organizations that provided resources for our shows' content; theaters and venues who offered reduced rates so we could bring our art and activism to the public; and funders that off-set production costs. They have all been thanked on our website and in our show programs, and I remain grateful to each of them. Poetic People Power would never have produced the shows included in this anthology or reached our 20th anniversary without their contributions and the many hundreds of people who attended our shows in New York City, at colleges, and at festivals.

And while space won't allow me to name everyone who has helped the project over the last two decades, I personally want to thank friends and family who supported me in this work throughout the years. This includes Ben Arredondo, Jim Buckmaster, Darren Molovinsky, Joe Gonzalez, Jacquette Timmons, Robin Stern, Melissa Mannis, Helen Churko, Wende Jager-Hyman, Karla Jackson-Brewer, Shetal Shah, Chris Gandin Le, Jennifer Jones, Michelle Ngo, Jennifer

Acknowledgments

van der Meer, Ragon Duffy, Ann Jablon, Joe Trentacosta, Jonathan Hemphill, Lynne Fisher, Kate Walbert, Frank La Frazia, Liz Zieminski, Magali Dupin, Becky Katzman, Jessica Slawson, Andrea Sparacio, Alyson Greenfield, Mark Rywelski, Erica R. DeLaRosa, Nikki Ortolani, Lyndsey Barratt, Melissa Fendell Moschitto, Dana Roc, Leeanne Schendel, Martha Neighbors, Ashley Faison, Jeanne Su, Susan Iekel, Ariel Field, Andrew Feigenson, Melinda Messineo, Kristen Schmidt, Lisa Butterworth, Rosa Trautz, Eric Jankiewicz, Frank Leone, Jeanie McElwee, Chris Bracco, Roseanne Bracco, Denis Bracco, Bonnie Tellez, Tom Tellez, Cassidy Tellez, Cody Tellez, and Carrie Bracco.

I believe deeply in the power of community work, and it's been a focus of my career. While I worked to amplify the voices of artists and present shows to advance social change, my community of friends and family gave me the support I needed to be a creative changemaker. I'm forever grateful.

POETIC PEOPLE POWER was founded in 2003 by writer Tara Bracco to create an ongoing project that combines poetry and activism. Now in its 20th year, Poetic People Power creatively explores social and political topics, offering insight and solutions to issues that affect our everyday lives. Using the expressive art of poetry, Bracco has presented 20 spoken work shows and commissioned 130 poems by 40 poets on timely topics, including climate change, the global water crisis, inequality, universal health care, pay equity, gentrification, time poverty, and human rights abuses.

Poetic People Power has received press in *O, The Oprah Magazine*, *Time Out New York*, *Poets & Writers*, *HuffPost*, *Insider*, *BroadwayWorld*, *Playbill*, and *Brooklyn Rail*, among other publications. Additionally, shows have been performed regionally at colleges (Columbia University, Stony Brook University) and festivals (Amnesty International Human Rights Art Festival and Art by the Bay Festival).

Art + Action = Change!

What art will you make?
What action will you take?

20 Shows, 40 Writers, 130 Poems Commissioned

poeticpeoplepower.com